Glenda's richly detailed
filled with beau
mountaintops a
sensory pleasure
narrative of slow   ...spiring
read but also a joy and pleasurable one.

Elizabeth J. Thompson, PhD candidate,
American Association of University Women Fellow,
University of Tulsa, Tulsa, Oklahoma

In Glenda Potts' book, you'll find a mature and sensitive spiritual guide who will open you to God's presence in everything and everyone. As we follow her beautiful prose and poetry that flow out of her spiritual journey, we learn her truth—that becoming aware of each new depth of God's presence requires new consent. From her life in God she shows that each new awakening changes our relationship to ourselves and to everyone and everything else. Helping people feel God's powerful presence is the purpose of this fresh, inspiring book.

Dr. J. Curtis Nigh, Minister/Therapist,
Oklahoma City, Oklahoma

With an eye admiring color and form, Glenda's prose and poetry invite us to gaze with her at God's creation. And with a heart aching for peace and joy, she lets us accompany her on her soul's journey to surrender to and love God.

The Reverend Janie Kirt Morris,
Emmanuel Episcopal Church, Houston, Texas

...tailed story of her journey to find a
... She takes the reader with her to ...dain
... and sandy beaches, all the while sharing the
... of experiencing God in the world. Her
...ly deepening faith is not only an inspira...

can you
feel *His*
powerful
presence?

*Rejoice in the peace
of His presence.*

Glenda Potts

Psalm 16:11

Poetic Reflections
of the Awareness of God

can you feel *His* powerful presence?

by Glenda Potts

TATE PUBLISHING & *Enterprises*

Published by Tate Publishing & Enterprises, LLC
127 E. Trade Center Terrace | Mustang, Oklahoma 73064 USA
1.888.361.9473 | www.tatepublishing.com

Tate Publishing is committed to excellence in the publishing industry. The company reflects the philosophy established by the founders, based on Psalm 68:11,
"The Lord gave the word and great was the company of those who published it."

Book design copyright © 2008 by Tate Publishing, LLC. All rights reserved.
Cover design by Janae J. Glass
Interior design by Steven Jeffrey

Published in the United States of America

ISBN: 978-1-60462-786-2
1. Poetry: Inspirational and Religious
08.01.24

Dedication

With deep appreciation I dedicate this book to the love of my life, my husband Kent, who has always been my greatest earthly encourager. Kent, who is my anchor and my lighthouse, has lovingly and patiently supported me from the first poem to the book's completion.

This book is also dedicated to my children—to my daughter, Diane, and her husband, Richard Green, to my son Stephen and his wife, Melinda, and to my son Gregory. I also devote this book to my grandchildren Seth, Nathaniel, Laree, and Meredith Green and Emily and Sophie Potts. My beloved children and grandchildren are each like a lovely and unique flower, which together form a beautiful bouquet that perfumes and enriches my life.

Further, I lift this book with love to the memory of my father, Lawrence Williams, and in honor of my mother, Waunita Williams, for their fine example of devotion to God, family, and farming. I also lovingly remember my dear sisters Carolyn Parker and Anita Melrose.

Above all, I consecrate this book to God, whose powerful presence and love inspired and encouraged these spiritual reflections. The invisible words of my soul, made visible by his unseen Spirit, allow me to express my gratitude to him for helping me laugh in the rain and smile in the dark. I am humbled by his power to encourage my mind to dance with hope, inspire my soul to sing with joy, and comfort my heart to be at peace whether the day is sunny or gray, as I choose to draw close to him and invite his loving presence.

Draw close to God, and God will draw close to you.
James 4:8

Acknowledgments

The author is only one of many people who are involved in creating a book. Although it isn't practical to list everyone, my gratitude goes to my family and friends who read poems or segments of this book and encouraged me to listen to my heart and share the insights of my faith journey. I am indebted to my niece Kathryn Kirt who proofread in the early stages. She encouraged me throughout the entire project and inspired me to envision myself as a writer.

I offer thanks to Elizabeth Thompson for her important guidance and expertise in proofreading. Thanks to Kay York Lierman and Bobbie Roe for making sage suggestions to improve the book. Many thanks go to those at Tate Publishing whose technical and creative expertise has been vital to the book's reality. Specifically, I appreciate the kindness and patience of Brianne Webb, who made the editing process a pleasure.

My appreciation goes to Dr. Norman Neaves, whose inspiring sermons and spiritual wisdom have influenced my insights and faith direction. I extend my gratitude to Dr. Curtis Nigh, whose theological expertise has contributed to my spiritual growth. I would also like to thank Rev. Janie Kirt Morris for her positive influence on my life and her encouragement to listen to the sacred whisper.

I wish to thank Kent Potts, Diane Green, Shirley Kelley, Mary Lu McEuen, and Carolyn Parker with heartfelt gratitude for pearls of wisdom, faithful encouragement, and treasured time as they honored their God-given gifts as encouragers and teachers.

Although it is intimidating to bare my soul and reveal my heart as an open book, I find the courage to do so through God's powerful love and amazing grace. Many times I felt like a pen in God's hands as I responded to a deep and compelling inspiration to write about encountering his powerful presence. My life has been wonderfully changed by the hope and peace I find in God. So it is with gratitude and love I wish to honor him with these faith reflections and poetic praises. It is my hope to inspire others to seek their own additional revelations and reflections about the glory of God as they ponder the profound and beautiful significance of his powerful presence.

Table of Contents

Foreword

You are in for a real treat—particularly if you allow yourself the time to really enter into these deeply personal and beautiful reflections of Glenda Potts. In fact, you might even discover yourself in this poignant disclosure of her soul and life's journey.

Most of us live our lives in very common and ordinary experiences, don't we? They come out of the daily routines and personal responsibilities that all of us have. And every once in a while, we have a special experience that lifts us up out of the sameness and daily grind of our common lives, but only occasionally do we have these special experiences and moments.

Glenda shows readers how the common, ordinary, and mundane experiences of our everyday lives can be seen through a different set of eyes and received through a different set of ears. A life lived at the ordinary level can actually be extraordinary when one discovers an invisible hand moving in those events. It can be transformed from a plain and ordinary life into one that is rich and full and incredibly meaningful. And that is possibly the most important thing that can transpire in any human being's life.

Do you remember the story of Moses when he was in the desert tending his father-in-law's sheep? Talk about a very plain and ordinary and uninspiring set of circumstances! And yet precisely there, in the midst of that hot and barren and terribly commonplace desert, Moses noted a bush aflame, and then he heard the voice of God speaking to him from that bush. It was the one single event that transformed his whole life and thrust him into the phenomenal leadership for which he would become so widely known. I wonder how many other people, if any, would have noticed that bush and actually discerned the whisper of God's voice coming to them from that bush.

And remember what the Voice said to Moses? "Take off your shoes, for the ground upon which you stand is holy ground."

Maybe the ground upon which you stand right now is also "holy ground." Not ordinary and plain and common after all. Not mundane and everyday and uninspiring, as we may have been led to think, but instead a place filled with sacred significance and meaning and thus "holy ground." Would it make a difference in your life were you able to see more deeply and to hear more discerningly? Would it make a difference if the plainness and ordinariness of your situation were to become "holy ground"?

Glenda is an extraordinarily sensitive person whose life journey I have been able to observe closely over the past thirty-five years. She doesn't live in a different world than the one in which you and I live. But over these last thirty-five plus years, I have watched her become increasingly aware of far more taking place in her world than she was able to realize a quarter of a century ago. She has become attuned to the profound spirituality of all of life, especially to the profound spirituality in her own personal life, and that is what she has courageously shared in these reflections you are about to read. I hope you will read them with eyes that have been transformed, with ears that are listening more deeply, and with a heart that is ready to enter into a new kind of spiritual awareness. The remarkable thing is not that she has experienced something that others of us haven't, but rather that through these courageous sharings out of her own soul, she has opened a door through which all of us may pass into a brand new and utterly vibrant experience. Maybe we are not finally human beings who every once in a while have a spiritual experience, but rather spiritual beings who right now are going through a human experience. And what a profound difference it makes when we come to that realization ourselves.

Dr. Norman Neaves
Senior Minister Emeritus
Church of the Servant (United Methodist)
Oklahoma City, Oklahoma

Introduction

I went in search of seashells; I found God's powerful presence. The sun of dawn had risen to a shining, bright height one particularly magnificent morning while I walked upon the shore, which skirted the daunting, though beautiful, ocean. The sunrays had turned the sea into an incredible shade of turquoise blue. Ocean breezes moved the palms in gentle rhythm with my breathing. The sugar white sand glistened from the sun's brilliance. Seagulls effortlessly sailed overhead through the warming ocean air. Midway between the shoreline and the horizon, dolphins jumped playfully. As the tide rolled in and out, little birds skittered over the beach in search of conch shells for sustenance. Soft sounds of laughter and conversation between fellow strollers filtered into my awareness. A rainbow in the cloudless sky formed a backdrop for this amazing natural setting. I walked, surrounded by God's awesome generosity, extraordinary power, and wondrous beauty. I felt his powerful presence.

His Powerful Presence

He smiled at me as he waved from a palm,

And steadied my heart with breezes of calm.

He walked beside me on the sandy shore,

Offering the treasure of his love to explore.

Strong currents of grace swept into control,

Washing courage over my fearful soul.

Hope billowing within like ocean waves

Filled me with joy for the path he paves.

My soul sang for the beauty of the earth,

And my heart danced in rhythm with the surf.

I watched in awe as waves flowed from the sea,

And felt his powerful presence set my soul free.

*"From there you will search again for the Lord your God. And if
you search for him with all your heart and soul, you will find him"
(Deuteronomy 4:29).*

The seaside is only one of countless natural settings that
provide us with the lovely experience of drawing into the
presence of God. God is available in nature, our life circum-
stances, and through all of his creations. We have only to
awaken to the presence of God and remember that above all
else he resides within our hearts.

An Initial Awareness of God's Presence

During a portion of my life I knew of God, but I did not know God. The accounts of God and creation in the Bible were introduced to me when I was a child in church. Every year in Sunday school, I heard the joyful Christmas story, recounting the miraculous birth of baby Jesus who brought love and peace into the world. Each spring I listened with sadness as the Easter story retold of the love in the sacrifice Christ made on the cross for us and the hope in his resurrection that followed. It was in Sunday school that I first sang "Jesus Loves Me" and memorized the Scripture John 3:16: "For God so loved the world that he gave his only Son, so that everyone who believes in him will not perish but have eternal life."

My church experience included strong sermons that were both confusing and uplifting. We sang beautiful and inspiring hymns about God that were deeply embedded within my soul. Occasionally I heard personal testimonies about the wonderful difference God's love and goodness were making for others. As a little girl, I responded to God's mysterious power with trembling awe, but I was unclear about its relevance for me. The stories of Jesus' love, goodness, and mystery stirred my imagination and planted subtle seeds of awareness that eventually blossomed into a hunger to learn more about him as Redeemer, Comforter, and Friend.

Mysterious Power

God may come to us in an amazing rainbow
Or in the flowing lyrics of a beautiful hymn.
We may sense his mystery in a shadowy garden
And when he moves morning light beyond dim.
His deity is manifested in the tiny hummingbird,
And his presence smiles down from the sun.
His power surrounds us with glorious splendor,
From dawn's first light until evening is done.
God is cradled in the vastness of the ebony sky,
Encouraging us from an unthinkable height.
His mellow moonbeams whisper to our hearts,
While his stars illuminate our souls in the night.
His unimaginable power is displayed in the ocean,
And his kindness comes in a gentle rain shower.
Miraculously, he knits us in mother's womb
And graces the wildlife of mountains that tower.
His goodness rests in the hearts of mankind,
And his generosity is in an implausible flower.
Our Supreme Savior reigns over the earth,
Forever in control with his mysterious power!

*"Yours, O Lord, is the greatness, the power, the glory, the victory, and the majesty. Everything in the heavens and on earth is yours, O Lord, and this is your kingdom. We adore you as the one who is over all things" (*1 *Chronicles* 29:11*).*

The reality of God was first impressed upon me through nature and the simple pleasures in life as I lived on the farm. In the wide-open spaces of the country, silence prevails and nature surrounds. Hosting only the birds of the air, the pure blue sky extends forever with an unobstructed view to the faraway horizon. The land consists of forests of trees, acres of crops, and plots of vegetables. Rivers, ponds, and lakes are sprinkled over the countryside and are home to fish and reptiles. Running water carves out ditches and ravines in the land. In the country, one finds a variety of untamed and domesticated animals, as well as both wild and barnyard fowl. Although the country bears an air of loneliness, there is a strong sense of another presence there—one that evokes peacefulness and hope. I was granted a glimpse of something profoundly larger than myself in this setting. My initial awareness of God's power and control and of his generosity, goodness, and love began when I was a child on the farm.

The success of our farm was vital to my family's livelihood. Moderate weather conditions were crucial to the quality of our farm crops. The survival of our farm animals was important. The ability of our cows to repeatedly produce healthy milk and the capability of our chickens to abundantly provide prime eggs were important factors in our farming triumphs. From my childish perspective, I understood the importance of sunshine and precipitation to the healthy life of our vegetable gardens. I realized the value of moderate weather and mild temperatures for the crops of wheat, alfalfa, corn, pecans, and maize to prosper. Each year the success of the field crops and vegetable gardens mattered greatly to my family.

God is everywhere in creation, and my life on the farm offered countless opportunities to experience the Creator. Sometimes in the twilight of a midsummer evening, a sense of peace enveloped me as I listened to the katydids sing and watched the sun disappear below the horizon. I often felt challenged by a great sense of mystery and awe, as I chased the intriguing fireflies into the darkness. Many warm summer nights I lay on a pallet of grass to gaze in amazement at the stars twinkling overhead. I held a sense of the earth's vastness close to my soul, if only for a moment. With fascination, I searched over and over for the friendly face of the "man in the moon" to smile back at me, and quite often he did.

The sun occasionally bathed me with more than physical warmth as I walked alongside our lakeshore under an azure sky that was adorned with a fleet of fluffy white clouds. Identifying the shapes in the clouds as they drifted slowly in and out of view heightened my wonder about the world around me. Squeezing mud between my toes on a country lane after a summer rain somehow gave me a sense of freedom, while a rainbow appearing magically overhead blessed me with an unidentifiable joy.

Fondly engraved in my mind are chilly autumn mornings of bright sunlight that highlighted the intricate frost designs etched overnight on our farmhouse windowpanes. The same frosty night visitors coated our lifeless lawn with a silver glaze that crackled underfoot. Certain autumn afternoons, as I returned home from school, a strong breeze moved a v-shaped collection of geese southward while the trees clutched colorful foliage. Many cold autumn Saturdays I helped gather the fruit of the pecan trees to earn money for Christmas gifts. The time spent in the pecan grove offered even more than money as I breathed the open air and listened to the birds chirping in the trees, cattle calling from the field, or dogs barking in the distance. Autumn was ripe with the promise of restoration for summer's surviving plants.

Winter followed autumn with a sense of God's warmth as I largely viewed the world from indoors. Loneliness pierces the winter silence as birds hush their singing and insects cease their chirping, but there is a presence in the cold, blowing wind and a greeting in the wet, delicate snowflake. The first snowfall of the season, drifting quietly and gently to earth, captured my fancy like little else ever did in my youth. I pondered the beauty and mystery in the gentle, yet obvious power that could magically transform the earth with a blanket of white. Happiness was mine through the magic of winter as I busily built a snowman, hurled a snowball, or knocked icicles from the roofline with my sisters. Whether I watched my daddy break through solid water for the cattle to drink or, on rare occasion, ice-skated with my sisters on our frozen farm lake, I often felt a mystical, invisible force was in control of life on the farm.

Hope visited my girlish heart again and again as night relinquished its reign to the dawn of a new day. On spring mornings the birds singing in the cedar tree outside my bedroom window expressed a sweet and contagious joy to be alive. Springtime's first blade of green grass gave rise to my hopes of shedding my shoes to walk barefoot outdoors after a long, cold winter. A yellow daffodil, a wild redbud, or a newborn calf helped signal the return of life each spring. Listening to strong spring storms whipping through the trees and whistling in the cracks of our farmhouse created a sense of the power and mystery in nature. Whether I cowered under the bedcovers while lightening pierced the darkness and menacing thunder followed or watched in awe while raindrops beat furiously upon the earth, I was aware of a surrounding, hidden energy.

The isolation of country life offered me the opportunity to ponder the world around me with a simple wonder. I pursued a toad, a turtle, or a grasshopper with great delight. I waited with a mixture of hope and boredom for a fish to pull under the bobbing red-and-white cork on my cane fishing pole. Daydreaming in the corn shed or jumping from haystacks were other pleasurable pastimes of mine. With an avid curiosity, I often strolled down the farm lane to retrieve the day's mail and make observations about the lazy cattle grazing in the pasture or the busy birds swooping from tree to tree. These explorations usually found me cocooned in contentment.

Freight trains rumbled daily over the steel tracks that stretched into infinity past our farm. I often ran with excitement to watch the train and wave at the conductor. Sometimes he would toot a "hello" as I hurriedly counted the railroad cars, eager to discover if this was the train that would be the longest one ever. I pondered the contents of the cars and the people within as it whistled toward a destination I could only imagine. One blustery winter day a freight train left a railroad tramp behind. I recall my mother not only provided him with food, but also, several large safety pins to hold his raggedy coat close around him. Although I initially felt concern about his ultimate intentions, my mother's compassion and kindness were impressed upon me that day. I was sad that he was homeless, cold, and hungry. On that gray day, as I felt his discomfort and loneliness, a subtle gratitude was instilled within me.

Danger lurked on the farm, or so it sometimes seemed. Fear, an uninvited guest, often accompanied me as I skirted the lakeshore where the water moccasins lived. I gave credit for any movement along the banks to the sneaky snakes. I was equally wary of the black chicken snakes as I explored the hay barn to play or entered the hen house to gather the eggs. I placed my hand into the nest with great trepidation, convinced a snake would bite me or a chicken would peck me. I felt relief each time I finished my task unharmed. The snakes and railroad tramps weren't the only reasons I had to be on guard—the unrestrained cattle often grazed nearby the path I routinely walked. Invariably the bull of the herd saw me as I hurriedly tried to slip by on my way to the mailbox, the vegetable garden, or the railroad tracks. Danger lurked on the farm, either real or within my mind.

Typically a time of beauty, springtime delivered unforgettable ugliness to our farm one year. On a cool Saturday morning in June my family was forced to flee on foot to safety as a nearby river overflowed its banks. The ordinarily placid river was raging from the many spring rains. It broke the levee around our farm and spread floodwaters over our crops. The river water stopped short one inch from entering our house. Life was altered that year as the crops were destroyed, roads were damaged, and spirits were dampened. The power and damage I observed were unfamiliar and frightening, yet somehow awe-inspiring.

Another springtime experience found me huddled with my family—and undoubtedly several snakes—in an underground shelter on a chilly, wet night while a funnel cloud spiraled angrily overhead. Targeting the home of my aunt and uncle in the next county, the tornado spared nothing except my aunt's beloved family Bible, which she took with her to the storm shelter. Their clawfoot bathtub found a new home many miles away in a Blackjack oak tree. These experiences heightened my awareness of a higher power.

My parents worked hard on the farm, but I recall idle hours that allowed for valuable bonding time with my family as we shared love, laughter, and tears. Lazy summer days, exciting autumn evenings, long winter nights, and invigorating spring mornings graced my life in the country. The summer months of activity, the autumn months of slowing, the winter months of restoration, and the spring months of reawakening were evident in the plant life on the farm. In many respects, the characteristics of the various seasons of the year were also evident in my life as my growth evolved in similar stages of activity, slowing, restoration, and reawakening throughout my childhood. My life on the farm was the foundation for my spiritual growth with the Creator. As I grew with a family who loved me and took me to church to learn about God, seeds of his love and his power were planted in my soul.

Planted Seeds

God's *power* in a lightning bolt split apart a tree,

And his *creativity* in a sunset was lovely to see.

His *gentleness* dwelled within the moon's mellow glow,

And his *glory* painted promises in a subtle rainbow.

His *joy* surfaced when the field crops thrived,

And *hope* returned as the gardens survived.

God extended his *grace* at the lakeshore to shield,

And his golden *majesty* waved in the wheat of the field.

His *greatness* was ordained in a brilliant blue sky,

And his *command* rode high in the clouds drifting by.

God *mercifully* relieved a drought with a shower,

And wild winds displayed his incredible *power*.

His *loyalty* nestled in sweet flowers of spring,

And his *joy* was audible as birds began to sing.

God's *miracle* was revealed when a cow gave birth,

And his *strength* was made visible as the calf met the earth.

He *graced* my life with wonderful parents to love,

And he sent sweet sisters, *generously* from above.

His *peace* cloaked my childish soul in a wooden pew,

And his *goodness* kept me safe from harm as I grew.

His *kindness* coated my world with tiny flakes,
And *majestically* spread a skating rink over the lake.
He *playfully* lit fireflies as dusk drew nigh,
And *faithfully* twinkled stars in an ebony sky.

> "Great is his faithfulness; his mercies begin afresh each day"
> (Lamentations 3:23).

In this poem my childish perspective of growing up on a farm consists primarily of idyllic recollections. However, life on the farm includes times of stress and difficulty as well as peace and simplicity. The ups and downs of farm life provide opportunities to learn about accepting what cannot be changed and how to remain grateful in spite of hardships and setbacks. A series of lessons on how to retain hope and persevere courageously are frequently available on the farm.

It is easy to be grateful when cattle are producing, chickens are prolific, or hogs are thriving on the farm. An abundance of alfalfa hay or a beautiful wheat field offers a sense of accomplishment. A healthy potato patch or a bumper pecan crop gives a reason for rejoicing. Moderate temperatures and appropriate precipitation are occasions for thankfulness. Peace reigns when life is simple and going well. There are many opportunities on the farm to experience the level of gratitude that will provide hope and produce joy.

It is difficult, however, to be grateful during times of crop failure or livestock loss on the farm. It is hard to accept the setbacks that are common in farm life. Discouragement rises from flooded crops and withered pecans. Disappointment reigns when vegetables freeze and wheat fields burn up. More than sadness settles in when crops fail or livestock die. Deep concern and fright often lead to despair during the various adversities that occur in farming. Hopelessness easily gains a foothold during difficult times on the farm. Farm life affords the time and opportunity to learn about patience, trust, and acceptance.

Regardless of where we live, over time life will likely bring challenges or sorrow our way. It is probable that each of us will eventually suffer discouragement, disappointment, or loss. Many of us find it difficult to face our trials with any remnant of hope. And certainly we cannot experience peace during our turmoil or joy during our sorrow. Or can we? Can we appreciate life after suffering a great financial loss? Or retain hope after a cancer diagnosis? Can we learn to smile through the pain of divorce? Or trust after betrayal? Can we persevere courageously instead of surrendering in the face of defeat? Is it possible to feel joyful when we are suffering the death of a dearly beloved? Or experience peace during conflict? Can we believe in tomorrow when doubting today? Can we maintain contentment when a beloved is held hostage by addiction? Or we are? Can we learn to let go of dreams and expectations and accept unsolicited or undesirable change? How can we find the courage and strength to graciously accept the uncomfortable or the unthinkable?

It is difficult to keep fear and doubt at bay during our trials. It is a challenge to avoid growing anxious during our hardships. These negative feelings of fear, doubt, and anxiety can unplug us at our core and drain us of joy, rob us of hope, and steal our peace. How do we protect ourselves against the thieves that would take away our joy and peace and remove our hope? How can we maintain our faith through illness or loss? How can we trade fear for faith and doubt for belief? Can we learn to persevere with courage through our trials? Can we find the strength to hold on tightly to our joy when harsh winds intermittently blow sorrow or trouble our way? Can we learn to tread the floodwaters of life that periodically ravage our lives and still return to the shore with hope intact and peace nearby? Is there a higher power with blessings that will buoy up our spirits, regardless of our trials? Is there an unseen source, available to us all, willing to love us through anything and strengthen us for our battles? Where will we find a guiding light of reassurance and comfort to combat the darkness?

"I look up to the mountains—does my help come from there? My help comes from the Lord, who made heavens and the earth!"
(Psalm 121:1–2).

We can choose to turn our eyes toward the Lord for help. We can seek the blessings of his nurturing love, mercy, and grace, his "manna from heaven," to help us withstand the complexities of life. We need his "heavenly manna" to help our hearts prosper and our souls thrive. We do not discover it alone. We do not happen upon his heavenly manna without the grace of guidance. We need a Guide to lead us to the soul food that fuels our faith and increases our trust. God our Creator and our Provider is that Guide. The same God who created us will provide for us. Our Creator, who gave us life out of profound love, will lead us to discover his blessings that offer a sustaining quality to our life journeys, regardless of a day's given destination. Whether we travel an exciting high road, a challenging low road, or a boring middle road, we will find hope and joy in his presence. On our journey in his presence we will discover his reassurance and encouragement is at every fork in the road to lead us to peace. Our Guide will provide fortifying hope whether the "farm" lives or dies. His manna from heaven leads to contentment.

As a child growing up on a farm, there were times I sensed a presence far greater than myself in charge and beckoning me. I developed an initial awareness of God in my childhood.

My Initial Awareness

My initial awareness of a powerful presence
Began in the country with countless clues.
After my childhood my vision grew dim
And I misplaced the hope in the Good News.
Far beyond the farm I wore a veil of bewilderment
And in a fog I watched from a distance, unsure.
Faded country images of his powerful presence
And childhood memories of his love grew obscure.
My initial awareness of God's presence,
Like a seed lying in wait in a dry garden,
Stirred in response to his living waters of love
And began to reach for the light in his pardon.

*"For if we are faithful to the end, trusting God just as firmly as when
we first believed, we will share in all that belongs to Christ"
(Hebrews 3:14).*

A Foggy Awareness
of God's Presence

After I left the farm I began to shift my focus inward. My initial awareness of God gradually diminished. I continued to go to church, but I did little else to nourish the seeds of God that were planted in my heart during childhood. The planted seeds lay dying under a foggy veil of uncertainty or indifference that shrouded them from light, vital for their growth. I did not permit myself to receive God's living waters of love, which would encourage the seeds to grow toward his light. Without his nurturing grace I was asleep to the possibility of strengthening the spiritual foundation that was formed in my childhood.

Whether my life was fraught with troubles or blissfully carefree, listlessness often filled my heart, leaving little room for hope. There were times when my soul should have been singing, but something intangible prevented a colorful expression of joy. Although I felt joyful in mountaintop moments, joy was absent in the valley times and infrequent on ordinary days. Regardless of the nature of my day, peace was often elusive as it was easily overshadowed by an unidentified restlessness. Positive feelings eluded me in the valley of worry. Fear robbed me of hope. Doubt crowded out joy. Anxiety absorbed my peace.

I longed for God's colorful rainbow of promises to appear through my troubles. I wanted to experience hope during trials. I needed the sunshine of his love to brighten my spirits during sorrow. I wanted to trust his joy to find me in the valley as well as on the mountaintop. Could I have faith that his peace could calm my anxious soul through anything? Could I receive the courage to persevere beyond fear and learn to let go of doubt? I longed for something specific to offer contentment in the midst of my life challenges. I wanted something intangible to make a profound and wonderful difference in the quality of my life. What could truly bring the richness of fulfillment in the middle of unfulfilling times? What could support and sustain me during my lifetime journey? Sometimes in a fog I recognized something vital was missing in my life. An important key to contentment evaded me. I observed people who seemed to have a secret path to consistent contentment regardless of their situations. What was blocking my path to contentment? Was something missing in my life?

God frequently came to me as company near dawn through the years of my foggy awareness as the planted seeds struggled to survive.

Company near Dawn

My Friend came again in the night
To return hope,
To encourage my trust,
And to teach me to cope.

To restore clarity,

To prepare me for a new day,

To remind me of faith,

And to show me the way.

To flood me with joy,

To provide new insight,

To portray peace,

And to inspire me to do right.

To offer me his love,

To release my trapped sigh.

Softly he tapped my soul awake

And entered my heart from on high!

"And he has identified us as his own by placing the Holy Spirit in our hearts as the first installment of everything he will give us" (2 *Corinthians* 1:22).

Upon reflection, I realize God offered me his grace during the years I created a home with my husband and children. Love and security were a part of my marriage. I remember the joy when I held my babies and their tiny fingers entwined with mine. I felt happiness over my children's achievements and hope during their growing pains. I received support from the love and thoughtfulness of my caring family and faithful friends. Gratitude and inspiration came to me through the kindness of a casual acquaintance or stranger. Interesting and uplifting family travels graced my life. Good health was one of life's greatest blessings. Life was good. Life was sweet. Life was full. Yet sometimes life felt bad, tasted bitter, or seemed empty, often for no apparent reason.

Through the years I occasionally entered periods of introspection and inquiry. What was my commitment to God when I received Jesus into my heart as a child? Did my confession of transgressions and God's forgiveness mean more than faithful church attendance? Is being a Christian simply about being a good person? Is it only about being honest and helpful? Is there something beyond simply believing in God? Through the years I often sang an old hymn, "What a Friend We Have in Jesus" and wondered how the words of the song applied to me. How could I find a friend in Jesus? Were the words to be taken to heart or simply to be sung ritualistically on Sunday mornings? What would it mean to have Jesus as my friend? Did I really need him? Why did I need him? What difference would it make to be friends with Jesus? What would be required to form a friendship with him? For that matter, what marks a meaningful friendship?

Someone once remarked that a true test of friendship is when two people are content to be together in silence. Few friendships could pass such a test without the initial ingredient of trust, which forms a bridge over which love can travel between two hearts. Over time love and trust reinforce the bridge to withstand the burdens and joys shared. Such a friendship is sacred. A relationship with God based on trust grows into a binding and sacred shared love.

We are often too lazy or selfish to spend the time or energy that is pertinent to the growth of a relationship. We may even believe we do not know how to begin one. We may feel incapable of encouraging the growth of a relationship or we may be unaware of the ingredients that would nurture a friendship. Sometimes we are not mindful of the potential for a relationship to be beautiful or worthwhile, as though we are asleep or in a fog.

For many years this is how I knew God. I knew him from a distance. I knew his name, but I did not know him. I knew a little about God, but I did not know his heart. I believed he did not know mine, simply because I did not share it. I was unaware of the beautiful blessings that awaited me in a personal relationship with God. I occasionally called on God when I needed help, but I was too impatient to spend time listening for him. I felt uncertain about how to properly communicate with God. Sometimes I was simply too lazy or indifferent. As though I was slumbering, I often maintained a foggy awareness of God's presence. Eventually my life would forever be changed; gradually, the fog would begin to clear as a stirring awareness began to grow within me that God is profoundly present everywhere in creation.

A Stirring Awareness of God's Presence in Nature

Even in a fog there were moments of a stirring awareness of God. I was often moved during Sunday morning sermons as the familiar words from my childhood about Jesus' transforming love and his profound sacrifice on the cross to atone for our sins filled me with hope. I was reminded of God's grace and power during the reading of the Scriptures. The hymns of sweet lyrics and moving melodies were inspiring. Singing the words of the beautiful hymns "Trust and Obey" or "Amazing Grace" stirred a conviction within me to follow God all the days of my life. But my focus was easily shifted from the cross to life's routine distractions during the weekdays. Outside the sanctuary the commitment seemed large. The possibility of being faithful to a relationship with Jesus felt daunting. I struggled in a fog from afar to understand what Christianity meant and how God's divinity applied to me. My acknowledgment of Jesus was casual; he was simply an acquaintance rather than my friend. I thought about

God, but, essentially, I did not feel his powerful presence. He waited.

God touched me in a variety of ways while he waited. He blessed me with the love of family and friends. I felt him as I witnessed the movement of life at weddings, funerals, and births. I heard him whisper my name in nature. He often called to me in the mountains or at the ocean. Sometimes I thought about God when I viewed the animals at the zoo or the plant life at a nursery. Occasionally, he visited me in my car, on neighborhood walks, or in various rooms of my house. Many times I felt a stirring awareness of God in my garden. Still, even as he surrounded me and waited to embrace me, I remained partially asleep to God's powerful presence. In my stirring awareness of God, as my life seemed full and good, I failed to focus on him long enough to connect with him personally. I failed to invite him to help me receive the level of hope and peace only he can provide. I turned my back on the joy that comes from knowing him. God came near, but I did not choose to draw near to him.

"Draw close to God, and God will draw close to you" (James 4:8).

Meeting God in the Garden

As a young woman, I discovered a love for gardening. The seeds about God that were planted in my soul during childhood were nourished in my backyard garden. Slowly they began to stir in response to his light. In retrospect I realize every spring and summer God revealed his face in the sweet roses, tiny pansies, and majestic hostas. The vibrant pink redbuds, stately red geraniums, and faithful yellow daffodils in my backyard awakened me to his presence time and time again. I caught glimpses of God's goodness and love in many different ways in nature, but most especially in my

backyard garden. His Eden array in my garden inspired a stir-
ring awareness of his magnificence.

An Eden Array

The softness of pinks blend to a purple allure
Amidst the yellows and the blues that abound,
And scarlet reds pose amidst the lily whites,
Garnishing the garden with beauty to astound.
Faithfully God restores spring growth,
Enhancing with color the tranquil scene.
He births little leaves from the bare gray limbs,
And paints tiny petals to soften the green.
A perennial amidst the Eden array
Rises proudly from the harsh winter soil
And magically presents a glorious surprise,
A faithful gift from the Creator's toil.
His offerings unearth my soul's restoration
And plant joy into my heart for a new day.
Indeed, God enhances my lovely garden,
Inspiring appreciation for his Eden array!

*"The Lord God placed the man in the Garden of Eden
to tend and care for it" (Genesis 2:15).*

Colorful, sweet-smelling flowers are a joyful delight and an
uplifting sight. With the proper nourishment, flowers flour-
ish to provide an amazing array of color tones that range from
tender pink to bright red, dusty blue to deep purple, and sun-

shine yellow to brilliant orange. Flowers display strength, perseverance, and beauty that warrant faithful attention. God reveals his love through the implausible flower.

The Implausible Flower

Much has been penned in prose
Of the daffodil, crocus, and rose,
And feelings have been written to rhyme
Of the lovely lily sublime.
The implausible flower of perfumed delight
Unfurls silky petals under heaven's light
And blooms in season with colorful precision,
Opening my mind to my soul's inner vision.
Strong perseverance, golden and bold,
Dwells at the center of the sturdy marigold.
And the striking tulip, so regal and tall,
Embraces my soul with glory to enthrall.
The fragile flower, elegantly pure,
Displays strength that will not endure.
God creates beauty in flower after flower,
Forever revealing his faithfulness and power.

"The grass withers, and the flowers fade, but the word of our God stands forever" (Isaiah 40:8).

I was happy during the years of my gradual awakening to God's presence, but I lacked special moments of jubilant joy that can only come from the Holy Spirit. I lacked God's level of hallowed hope and perfect peace. I allowed regrets, disappointments, and challenges in my life to perpetuate my unawareness of him. While I often recognized God, I was primarily aware of him from a distance. I felt unsure of God's love and his availability to me. I left him tending the flowers in my back garden while I went indoors to tend to myself alone. Although I believed, I wasn't listening closely enough to hear God's gentle whisper.

A Gentle Whisper

Arousing the crickets to chirp at dusk,
Stilling the birds of the darkening air,
And sealing the cracks of a wounded heart
Is a gentle whisper of tender loving care.
Comforting the lonely, fearful, and aged,
Calming the sweet soul of a child in distress,
And offering new hope to the searching soul
Is a reassuring, gentle whisper to bless.
Dwelling within each laborious gait,
Encouraging the battling spirit of the ill,
And inside each soul struggling to believe
Is a gentle whisper of the Lord's perfect will.
Bowing patiently in silence before the Lord
Reveals his sacred messages so dear.
His gentle whispers of hope, peace, and joy
Come when we humbly seek and revere.

"My child, listen to me and treasure my instructions. Tune your ears to wisdom, and concentrate on understanding" (Proverbs 2:1–2).

A sense of God's peace enveloped me on mild, sunny days in my garden as butterflies flitted amidst the flowers. I felt awe as a ladybug found a home on my arm. And the birds added to the awareness that God is ever-present. I surely knew something far greater than I was near and in charge, whether a bright red cardinal was singing an early morning greeting to his mate, a bluebird was chirping "hello" midday, or a mockingbird was warbling goodnight with a joyful tune. As I encountered God in my garden, the seeds planted in my soul long ago on the farm were beginning to stir to life.

God Is in My Garden

There is a feeling I feel so strong:

God is in my garden; I know I'm not wrong.

He's in the delicacy of the pansy so fragile,

He's in the roots as they spring back to life,

He's in the soil providing nutrition,

And in the soft rain relieving dry strife.

He's in the green grass that carpets each spring,

He's in the strength of the trees that tower,

He's in the shrubs with their delicate leaves,

And in the miraculous bulb, birthing a flower.

He's in the leaf beginning to unfurl,

He's in each blossom of floral delight,

He's in the branches seeking to sprawl,

And he's in the vine growing to the light.

Yes, the Master Creator lives in my garden,

Whispering to me when I make my rounds.
Indeed he's in my garden, for I feel his presence
Reigning over the life and beauty that surrounds.
There it is again, a feeling so strong:
God is in my garden; I know I'm not wrong!

"Then the Lord God planted a garden in Eden, in the east, and there he placed the man he had created" (Genesis 2:8).

———

Spending time digging in the soil to tend the flowers temporarily fed an unidentifiable hunger in my heart and watered an unquenchable thirst within my soul. The sunshine nurtured my body while gardening nourished my heart and soul. I often sensed a presence far greater than myself while tilling the earth of my garden.

The Presence of Sweet Peace

While in the green haven of my backyard
God bequeathed to my soul sweet peace.
His beautiful flowers under the majestic trees
Allowed my captive tears to seek release.
He whispered to my sad heart grown aware,
"Give all your sorrow to me, my dear child,
Seek relief from your troubled thoughts
And hear whispers of peace, soft and mild."
So, beneath the boughs of towering trees,
With exquisite flowers nearby my feet,
I felt the presence of the Lord's sweet peace

Embracing my victories and dispelling defeat.

"The Lord gives his people strength. The Lord blesses them with peace"
(Psalm 29:11).

Some days I spent hours working and relaxing in my backyard. I found it difficult to walk away, as though I would be abandoning a peaceful presence responsible for my temporary joy. The flowers possessed vibrant colors that seemed to be absent from my soul. They faintly whispered a special message of courage and hope. Underlying my moments of inspiration in the garden was a restlessness and conviction that, indeed, something vital was missing in my life.

A Beautiful Place of Inspiration

In the garden, clad with dewdrops at dawn,

When the Creator lights his powerful lamp,

He waits amidst the beautiful flowers,

Whose pretty petals cradle heaven's damp.

He comes to grace the lovely space

Amidst fragrant flowers of my garden,

And his gentle breeze softens my regrets

While his graceful green grants a pardon.

The rising sun filters through trees

Spreading warm rays over the pansies below,

And the soft morning light inspires me to reflect

On the Creator, whom I'm longing to know.

Yes, in the garden, where the dear Lord dwells,

He'll guide me to renounce the troubled night.

I can fling away all my sorrow in rhythm

With his dancing shadows and sweet, lilting light.

A place to go, a beautiful place of inspiration

Where I can feel his presence dwelling for hours,

Is in the garden where his love encourages,

Extending the grace he generously showers.

"He will lead them to the springs of life-giving water. And God will wipe away all their tears" (Revelation 7:17).

Experiencing the Lord through His Heavens

The Lord's kindness is in the heavenly moisture that invigorates the plants. We feel his inspiration as raindrops sparkle on a leaf in the sunshine or the green of the lawn is enhanced by a shower bath. We are in awe as the colorful rainbow emerges from gray clouds to remind us of his promises. His goodness is in the sweet, soft spring rain that revitalizes the earth.

Soft Spring Rain

A soft spring rain delights my soul

Like taste buds thrill over sweet cream.

Revitalizing raindrops from heaven

Sugar my heart like a dear, cherished dream.

I gaze into a rain-streaked windowpane

And see the glorious gift of a cool, rainy day.

The Lord cleanses my soul of clinging soot
And sprinkles the plants to keep thirst at bay.
The rhythm of raindrops satiate my heart
And lift my spirit like my husband's gentle kiss.
The Lord's goodness in raindrops from heaven
Delivers a love exceeding everyday bliss.

"I will thank the Lord because he is just; I will sing praise to the name of the Lord Most High" (Psalm 7:17).

Nature's power is as awe-inspiring as her gentleness. We sense God's mystery as lightning splits the darkened sky and rumbling thunder resounds in our ears. His kindness reigns as frenzied winds pelt raindrops onto a thirsty earth. We see his generosity as the rivers and lakes refill. We experience God's power through the mighty thunderstorms.

Heaven's Storms

The power in the thrashing winds we cannot see
Releases the raindrops from heaven to pour free.
The moisture in the howling air turns into ominous hail
And awakens us to a providence that'll always prevail.
Threatening storms turn us toward a divine design
As slashing light brings foreboding hard to define.
Heaven's storms remind us how powerless we are
While God's mighty love not even the storms can mar!

"The voice of the Lord echoes above the sea. The God of glory thunders. The Lord thunders over the mighty sea" (Psalm 29:3).

Our boundless God displays tremendous power in the mighty roar of nature's storms and he spreads his gentle generosity in the silence of an elegant snowfall. The beauty of joy drifts slowly from the heavens that are pregnant with God's incomparable peace.

Pregnant with Peace

Cascading from on high, little snowflakes,

Whiter than a cloud on a bright blue day,

Move me to smile as heaven's white splendor

Gently lifts my cares and doubts away.

Pregnant with peace, the gray sky releases

Joy for my heart while adorning the earth.

Warm feelings enter my being

When the heartbeat of heaven gives birth.

"No wonder my heart is filled with joy, and my mouth shouts his praises!" (Psalm 16:9*).*

I encountered God outdoors in a variety of ways. Even in partial slumber I was aware of God's creative work in nature. His power was in the rising sun and his beauty in its colorful glow. I felt his joy and peace in the faithful morning sunshine lighting another brand-new day.

The Serenity of Morning Light

Sitting in reflection on my garden bench,
Bathed in the serenity of morning light,
Captured was I by the rosy pink hues
Spreading softly over the blue and white.

My little feathered friend in red,
Resting beside me in a frozen perch,
Shared in the stillness of early worship,
A poignant moment in my silent search.

Safely reposed, surrounded by peace,
Absorbing the light that conquered the night,
Hope rekindled for the day underway,
And sent my anxiety on a one-way flight.

The Lord's faithfulness in the morning light,
Joyful evidence of his goodness and power,
Spreads his colorful love over the earth,
To reign beyond the time of the sunrise hour.

"Understand, therefore, that the Lord your God is indeed God. He is the faithful God who keeps his covenant for a thousand generations and constantly loves those who love him and obey his commands" (Deuteronomy 7:9).

I sensed his peace descending at day's end as the setting sun dimmed the view of my backyard domain. He spread his glorious hope in the twinkling stars of night as their familiar patterns dressed the blackened sky. I marveled at his faithful creativity as the moonlight silently bathed the lawn and flowerbeds with a soft, comforting glow. God inspired me to follow the light of his love through his miraculous array of heavenly lights.

Heavenly Delights

God sends sunny hope from dawn until night,

And sparkles his joy through heavenly delights.

Tiny bright lights expose new schemes

And magic moonbeams dust our dreams.

Peacefully hidden beyond mind or eye,

From dawn to dawn he guides from on high.

Reigning over the earth in a twinkling star,

Glittering with glee from his heaven afar.

Sending his mercy from celestial heights,

Glowing his grace through heavenly delights,

His bright rays of hope spread peace to console

And his warm light of love reflects joy untold.

"The sun has one kind of glory, while the moon and stars each have another kind. And even the stars differ from each other in their beauty and brightness" (1 Corinthians 15:41).

Receiving the Holy Spirit in the Mountains

God's awesome presence prevails throughout the earth. He is in nature's precipitation, throughout heaven's galaxy, and within the plant life of our gardens. His majesty is in the gentle meadows and towering mountains. He prevails over the peaks of green that rise from the valley to pierce the fluffy white clouds. His beauty is visible in the cascading cedars and tall pines of the mountains. His power is audible in the roaring water. His strength is in the foaming white rapids that engulf huge boulders and briefly conceal them from view. His energy swiftly propels a rubber raft through the raging river and delivers it through a formidable gorge.

God's touch is prevalent in the mountains. Sweeping panoramic vistas host majestic evergreens in every direction. Towering blue cedars and green pines cling courageously to steep slopes and provide a refuge for wildlife. The trees, often glistening with snow, offer a lovely perch for the birds. God's majesty is visible in the brave wildlife, pristine beauty, and enduring plant life. The Holy Spirit abounds in the mountains.

Sovereign Spirit

A strong, strong Spirit rustles in the pines
And in ghosts hovering in antiquated mines.
Pouring over boulders bathed in the light,
A Spirit dances in sparkling waters of white.
Swimming in the rivers of salmon and trout
Or painting wild pastures is a Spirit devout.
Bubbling with joy in an ice-cold brook
Is a breath of compassion we mustn't overlook.
Ruling majestically over a lofty mountain peak
Is a sovereign Spirit we're created to seek.
The same divine presence in the valley below
Offers our hearts a profound love to know.

"You formed the mountains by your power and armed yourself with mighty strength" (Psalm 65:6).

———————————

This powerful Spirit was generous with color while I visited the mountains. Fields of beautiful wildflowers waving yellow, orange, red, purple, and blue were a marvel to behold. As we ascended into the mountains, this incredible carpet of interwoven color could be seen peeking through a snowfall. In the purity of the snow-covered mountain peaks embraced by a brilliant blue canopy, I recall God whispering, "How can you overlook my powerful presence in such loveliness and serenity?"

Seeking the Heavens

Towering green pines, seeking the heavens,

Harbor sacred secrets only the wind can know.

Hosting an array of wild birds in green boughs,

They nod peacefully to the wildflowers below.

Nurturing the evergreens to sing with joy,

Grounding their roots to dance with hope,

Heaven's astonishing bright light

Shines love to the trees of the slopes.

Embracing the green needles of the pines,

Providing thirst-quenching nectar to sip,

Is the generosity of a heavenly Spirit

Showering joy and peace into each little tip.

"You will live in joy and peace. The mountains and hills will burst into song, and the trees of the field will clap their hands" (Isaiah 55:12).

Yes, God waits with joy at the top of the mountain where the air is thin but sweet and pure. He dwells at the pinnacle where peace from his splendor envelops our souls. The wildflowers sing with joy as God smiles his love through his warming sunrays. The birds reverently hush as though inviting his whisper. The deer trustingly bow to nibble in his peace. Gray skies, turbulent clouds, and rising winds cannot conceal God's heavenly presence. Rather, they serve to remind us of him and the everlasting hope that lies in his faithfulness.

"Yes, there will be an abundance of flowers and singing and joy! The deserts will become as green as the mountains of Lebanon, as lovely as Mount Carmel's pastures and the plain of Sharon. There the Lord will display his glory, the splendor of our God" (Isaiah 35:2).

Sensing God in Ocean Settings

God's natural creations are abundant in the hidden forests, golden plains, and arid deserts. His works are prevalent in the humid rain forests and lush green valleys. The beautiful seashores, the mighty oceans, and the treasures of the sea display their own unique power, beauty, and faithfulness. Our Creator fuels our awareness of his powerful presence and inspires us to new heights as we focus on the mystical beauty of his ocean settings.

Fuel for Inspiration

My eyes feast upon the royal blue ocean,
Caressing the border of white sand.
My soul embraces the blue sky above,

And ponders the mysteries of the land.

The ocean teems with hidden life

While seagulls sail visibly overhead.

My heart lurches as waves recede

And hungry sandpipers seek to be fed.

The sea churns its captivating colors

As a friendly dolphin playfully waves.

My mind marvels at the beautiful creations

And the wondrous scene on my heart engraves.

God's limitless love, fuel for inspiration,

Extends deeper than the depth of the sea.

The Lord's infinite control of my destiny

Washes waves of anticipation over me!

"If you look for me in earnest, you will find me when you seek me"
(Jeremiah 29:13).

A strong sense of God's presence enveloped me in ocean settings. When the sun was barely free of the horizon I strolled along the sea's lovely shoreline and sensed his hope and joy. The lip of the ocean spit playful waves across the sand. I received a sense of God's power and a sample of his gentle nature as the seawater rolled across my feet. A wondrous feeling of God's peace prevailed on my seaside walks whether I was pursuing little treasures of broken coral and seashells or observing a mysterious fog shrouding the sea on a misty morning.

The Veil

Slowly, the veil stealthily creeps,

Concealing visions of peace, minor and grand.

Mysteriously, the veil hides familiar realms

And rolls joyless doubt over the land.

Obscuring reality, a blanket of gray

Heavily enshrouds the deserted beach.

Dark fear slithers through the thickness,

Creating a sense of hope beyond reach.

Quietly, hope returns to the eye of the soul

As darkness yields to the powerful sun.

Victory prevails over the veil,

And life revives when faith has won!

"He made the things we can see and the things we can't see"
(Colossians 1:16).

God is responsible for the swaying palm trees that dot the seashores. The green fronds of the palms wave against a backdrop of blue sky and turquoise sea while the sun highlights the incredible colors. As the sun retires at dusk, the same palm fronds gently cast black silhouettes across a vast canvas of silver and gray. The sun slowly sinks into the ocean and paints the sea and sky with breathtaking shades of glorious pink and captivating orange. God paints his glory with the brilliant colors of a sunset over the sea's surface for our eyes to behold his beauty and our souls to wonder at his power.

Unfolding Glory

Leading the pallid sea to speak,

Reflecting color on the white clouds residing,

God bathes the sky with orange and pink tones,

Painting messages gloriously abiding!

Displaying magnificent color at day's end,

Creating a masterful show,

His scene full of glory dips quickly into the sea,

Touching my heart with its lovely warm glow.

God spills his golden tones over the ocean gray

Using rose red and bright pink to blend.

He swiftly paints his masterpiece into my heart,

And my soul exclaims his joy beyond the sunset's end.

The unfolding glory of a spectacular sunset

Presents the Creator's ballad without voice.

Painting a picture over the canvas of the sea,

His artistry colors my heart to sing and rejoice!

*"In a great chorus they sang, "Holy, holy, holy is the Lord Almighty!
The whole earth is filled with his glory!" (Isaiah 6:3).*

The ocean waves rhythmically erased my footprints and peacefully soothed my soul one morning as I meandered along an expanse of creamy white sand in search of seashells. The seagulls soared serenely overhead in a bright blue sky filled with gentle sea breezes. Suddenly, appearing mid-way between the shore and the horizon, an incredible creature thrust upward from the ocean's wild turbulence of sparkling colors. I watched in awe as a humpback whale swam with incredible power while the ocean's emerald green color was enhanced by the sun's extravagance. At the ocean's edge, I stood marveling at God's omnipotence. His beauty and generosity amazed me.

I observed God's strength in the power of the pounding surf as it coated the ancient black lava rock white with sea foam. The ocean fed my soul with waves of love as they returned unceasingly to the seashore.

Waves of Love

Ocean waves in continuous motion,

Churning and crashing forevermore,

Faithfully return a radiant emerald green

Or an intense royal blue to the awaiting shore.

Bearing the faithfulness of spring's return

And the power of summer rays so bold,

The waves race color to the endless shores,

Cresting a sea scene lovely to behold.

Faithfully God splashes joy into each heart,

Pouring out goodness to far reaches of the land.

Washing waves of love deeper than the ocean's floor,

His grace of hope and peace remain close at hand!

"Praise the Lord! Give thanks to the Lord, for he is good! His faithful love endures forever" (Psalm 106:1*).*

My gray mood matched the color of the ocean as I walked along the shore. A slight chill in the air invaded my body and penetrated my soul. The colorless setting discouraged peace from finding a place in my mind and checked hope at the door of my heart. Joy vacated my soul to make room for my woes. While I pondered my current challenges, without warning, a school of dolphins surfaced playfully from the lackluster sea to brighten the bleak atmosphere. Their fun and entertaining frolic returned life to the sea and to me. The dolphins quickly diverted my feelings from mild dejection to strong delight. Their antics brought levity to my cloudy mood, reminding me that God has an abundance of ways to bring joy into our difficult situations. All the while, during my contrasting seaside experiences, countless creatures swimming in the depths of the enormous sea, flying overhead in the endless sky, and inhabiting the immense land were thriving, oblivious to God's power to orchestrate life.

With peaceful feelings I glimpsed a part of God's gentle and loyal nature through the ocean's compelling ebb and flow.

Ebb and Flow

Slowly the foamy waves ebb and flow,

Dancing their whitecaps over a turquoise floor.

Rolling closer with playful peacefulness,

The salty sea seeks the secluded shore.

Faithfully, ocean waves flow toward land

Curling to and fro in fascinating roll.

Competitively the waves target the shore

Rhythmically returning to their ultimate goal.

Whitecaps tipping the beckoning sea waves

Wash a purifying joy into the core of me.

An awareness of the Lord's faithfulness
Surfaces with the swells of the emerald green sea.

"All heaven will praise your miracles, Lord; myriads of angels will praise you for your faithfulness" (Psalm 89:5).

I experienced God's splendor in the tropics where majestic waterfalls plummet past abundant flora. The falls gingerly mist bamboo, ferns, and philodendron vines while en route to foaming pools far below. Blossoms shift in the breeze and emit a scent of perfume. Lush lavender orchids dangle their glory from crevices in black lava rock. The rouge red hibiscus blooms proudly dress the landscape. Plush purple bougainvillea bushes gloriously blanket the slopes. I saw God's amazing versatility in the striking red poinsettia bush, the exotic bird of paradise flower, and the football-shaped pod of the cocoa tree. I felt his presence as I was surrounded by his beautiful creations.

Absorbing God in Nature

Our Creator abounds in his world of natural beauty. He lovingly crafted the earth with majestic mountains, awesome canyons, and vast valleys. He created the powerful oceans, pristine lakes, and meandering rivers. He spread the earth with rolling hillsides, sweeping plains, and green pastures. God gave us the gifts of tropical rain forests and beautiful gardens. We experience God's hope, peace, and joy in nature. Our Master's creations are for upholding, sustaining, and enhancing life here in his earthly realm. And surely these earthly wonders are only lowly glimpses of those that await us in God's heavenly realm of eternal life.

Earthly Wonders

Majestic mountains shadow the valleys,

And meandering rivers flow gently into the sea.

Golden plains recollect the pioneer's brave hope,

And butterflies in the wildflowers flutter free.

The seashores flaunt endless ribbons of sand,

And beautiful blue oceans wave with grace.

Jungles of green provide an animal haven,

And fair flowers enhance our earthly space.

The ocean breezes waft joy into our songs,

And the strength in the wind encourages belief.

Breathtaking sunsets color our senses,

And spectacular sunrises offer relief.

The rainfall quenches the thirst of the earth,

And the sunshine empowers creation to grow.

Shining subtly over the nocturnal,

The celestial lights emit a soft holy glow.

We live in an incredible world

Where amazing earthly wonders abound.

Joy and hope are inspired through creation

And peace is in the beauty all around.

"Then God looked over all he had made, and he saw that it was excellent in every way" (Genesis 1:31).

How can we not recognize God's excellence when the royal blue of the ocean meets the bright blue of the sky and we see not the end of either? How can we remain unaware of God's unending power when we ponder the unfathomable depth of the raging sea and the unimaginable distance to his heavenly arena? How can God's sovereignty go unrecognized when we are in awe of the height and splendor of the majestic mountains or the depth and mystery of the cavernous valleys? How can we fail to experience God's joy in rainbows that dip colorfully into the turquoise sea, appear magically from towering mountains, or spread gloriously over the golden plains? How do we miss his majesty and peace in the star-studded blackness of the night sky? And what of his magnificent hope as the world is lit by the powerful sun by day and the soft glow of moonbeams by night?

Many of us are aware of the wondrous mystery and beauty in nature but fail to give God the credit. We seldom acknowledge his existence in creation on a conscious level. If we do become aware of God, we often move beyond our feelings and our experiences to maintain our distance. We seldom awaken long enough to fully acknowledge God's presence. Nor do we choose to draw close to him during snippets of awareness even though he waits to receive us.

When

When loneliness overcomes you,
Gaze into the eyes of a star.
When sorrow tries to pursue you,
Know my love I send from afar.
When emptiness envelops you,
Whisper your need to the wind.
When joy is frozen inside of you,
Feel the hope in the sunshine I send.

When discouragement seems to cling,

Seek my peace as sunbeams color the sky.

When you've forgotten how to sing,

Let the soft moonbeams help you try.

"Both day and night belong to you; you made the starlight and the sun"
(Psalm 74:16).

———————————

For a long time I did not understand that God would gladly embrace me if I would claim his presence and invite his grace to sustain me. I failed to realize our Lord would fulfill my longing for that which I was unable to name. I ignored God's power to replace my gloomy disposition with hope. I overlooked my Savior's ability to calm my restlessness with his peace and fill the empty spaces of my soul with his joy. I did not comprehend that God was waiting to draw close to me.

Awakening to God's Presence through Our Senses

Seeing the Majesty of God in His World

God is, indeed, everywhere. The opportunities to see God in any given day are as seemingly incessant as the beating of a tiny hummingbird's wings. We see God in countless ways in nature. We see him in the lifecycle of the plants. We see him repeatedly in the behavior of animals and insects. He can be seen in the faithfulness of the domesticated dog, the courage of the ferocious lion, and the beauty of the graceful giraffe. God's glorious details can be seen in the spider working on his intricate home, in the bee flitting from flower to flower seeking nectar, or in the trail of ants displaying a preordained purpose in their movements.

Could you create a list of the ways you see the majesty of God in creation? Would your list include the simple things of life as well as the profound? Would your list include the mundane as well as the inspiring? Would your list surprise you as you ponder the amazing availability of God through your sense of sight? Our lists would be dissimilar, as we each see and experience God differently.

We can draw into God's presence through our senses as we see, hear, touch, taste, or smell him in our world around us. We can especially experience God through our sense of sight during each season of the year as he restores in the winter, renews in the spring, produces in the summer, and transitions in autumn.

Winter's Respite

Birds hush their warbling during winter rest
And seek refuge when harsh winds blow.
Weary plants retire in cold winter soil
And relax their roots in deep sleep below.

Wearing winter's pristine white coat,
Moaning in the chilly wind, naked and gray,
Yesterday's sprawling branches of color
Pine for the promise of a warm spring day.

Awaiting new life in winter's respite,
Dormant bulbs lie hidden in the garden or glen.
Seemingly without a purpose or goal,
The plants prepare to exhibit color again.

Weary from the busy growth of summer,
Abandoning autumn for the season of refuel,
The plants receive peace in winter's respite
And anticipate birthing a brand new jewel.

*"He lets me rest in green meadows; he leads me beside peaceful streams.
He renews my strength. He guides me along right paths, bringing
honor to his name" (Psalm 23:2–3).*

Spring's Rebirth

Spring draws nigh with a hopeful sigh,
Inspiring gray, barren branches to sprawl.
Unfurling fragile green leaves, the trees
Bedeck their limbs until autumn's recall.
Tuned in to the Master Gardener's revival,
Perennials wait in the prelude of rebirth.
Renewed to return to spring's center stage,
The flowers rise from the bowels of the earth.
Rested roots push fresh shoots upward,
Ready to embrace spring's slight chill.
Prepared to preen the green of spring,
Plants follow the Creator's plan and his will.
Awakening from a deep winter sleep,
Signaling the end of winter's long reign,
The birds celebrate spring's rebirth,
As they warble God's joy to proclaim.

*"You will show me the way of life, granting me the joy of your presence
and the pleasures of living with you forever" (Psalm 16:11).*

Summer Offerings

Newborn leaves grow to perfect prime,
Flourishing in the warmth of the summer season.
Entangled vines spread in an unrivaled frenzy
And deliver an array of blossoms beyond reason.
Life beaming down through magical sunrays
Creates a proud pinnacle of beauty that shows.
Displaying bold glory in the summer array,
God nourishes the color he generously bestows.
The prolific season enlivens my spirits
With a unique and bold beauty I admire.
Splashing his color amid the green foliage,
The Lord's summer offerings move me to aspire.

*"You set the boundaries of the earth, and you make
both summer and winter" (Psalm 74:17).*

Autumn

Brightly painted petals dress the pansies
And flutter in the breeze on autumn days.
Orange pumpkins contrast with purple violas,
Nestled amidst hay bales in a golden haze.
Delivering a scene in autumn's transition,
The Creator rests his power in a colorful scheme.
He highlights the foliage with yellow and gold,

And vivid orange and red emblazon the green.

Painting the leaves from a colorful palette

And covering the morning with a silver chill,

God ushers autumn from a prolific summer

Into the winter respite of his perfect will.

"There is a time for everything, a season for every activity under heaven" (Ecclesiastes 3:1).

Reverence for God and his power settles into our souls as we view him in nature. We revel in the rainfall, we marvel at the sunshine, and we ponder the miracle of a tranquil snowfall. We see the Creator's kindness in the peace of the glistening snowflakes. Each unique snowflake reveals the Creator's loving generosity and mystical beauty.

A Tranquil Snowfall

I am in awe of a tranquil snowfall

Coating the bare branches wintertime white.

Tiny glistening snowflakes of pure peace

Float silently into the stillness of the night.

I ponder the purity of the driven snow

Bearing a flawless love that frees.

The drifting sheets of sparkling crystals

Create a scene of contentment to seize.

I am enchanted with the magical snowflakes

Tumbling with life through dreamlike space.

Quietly turning the grayness into white bliss,

They gift with a layer of beauty and grace.
I receive the Creator's impeccable love
In the peacefulness of a snow shower.
The blessings within a tranquil snowfall
Drift into my heart and gently empower.

*"I lay down and slept. I woke up in safety, for the
Lord was watching over me" (Psalm 3:5).*

Visually, we receive the gifts of God's majesty in many ways
through nature. We see the snowflake in the wonder of win-
ter. We see the colorful, tender blossoms of the redbud beauty
in the splendor of spring.

The Redbud Beauty

Gazing from my bedroom window
One bright morning in the fresh face of spring,
I saw a sample of God's splendor and grace
In a tree so lovely my soul opened to sing!
Standing boldly upright with majestic color,
Redbud branches, yesterday empty and gray,
Wore an abundance of petite purple flowers,
Enlivening my heart to open and pray.
The tree blossoms of exquisite beauty,
A visual blessing of wondrous delight,
Regally unfolded when a soft spring shower
Dripped heaven's generosity into the night.

"Great is his faithfulness; his mercies begin afresh each day"
(Lamentations 3:23).

Hearing the Goodness of God through Creation

We encounter God in many different ways through our sense of hearing. We each have our own personal sound memories that enlighten us about God in nature. We can hear God in the aggressive wind or in the rattling hail. We can hear his power in the roar of the ocean, his kindness in the flutter of wings, or his gentleness in the whispering breezes.

The Winsome Wind

When flowers frolic in spirited dance,

I hear the joy in the winsome wind,

And I hear the courage in rippling leaves,

Clinging to the trees with life to defend.

When welcome raindrops appear in a cloud,

I hear hope in the winsome wind,

And I hear the strength in unleashed currents

Directing the towering trees to bend.

I hear compelling peace challenging me to grow

Floating in the strands of the winsome wind,

And I hear a sovereign whisper winging through the air

Inspiring me to sing to my best friend!

"You make the clouds your chariots; you ride upon the wings of the wind. The winds are your messengers" (Psalm 104:3–4).

We experience the Creator through our sense of hearing beyond the world of nature. Voices lifted harmoniously in song or spontaneously in laughter touch us in a joyful way. We are moved by the power of a rousing symphony. He touches us through hands on a keyboard or as a bow brings life to a violin. The sounds of soldiers marching to drums or voices joined in singing our country's national anthem bless us on some profound level as we sense the Creator's divine presence. We can feel God as we listen to mournful bugle taps at the funeral of a fallen countryman. We can hear him in the uplifting sounds of a harp at a beautiful wedding. God blesses us as he enters our sense of hearing in countless ways.

Come Listen for God's Whisper

Listen for God's whisper, kindhearted and mild,
Calming at dusk the wee birds of the air.
Listen to a mother soothing her child
And you'll hear his sensitive, loving care.
Listen for his spirit in the coo of the dove
And hear him as he rustles in the leaves.
Listen for him in nature's noises of love
And as his rowdy rain peppers a breeze.
Listen for God through laughter and tears,
And listen for him when he's raised in song.
Listen for his whisper in your heart's inner ear,
Uplifting you when your day has grown long.
Listen for God in your mother's sad sigh,
And listen to your brother's heart with care.

Listen for sweet charity in a gentle lullaby,

And listen for him in the silence of prayer.

Come listen to the message he sends you today

With an open heart, fresh ears, and alert mind.

Come listen to what the Lord has to say.

Listen quietly to what he would have you find.

*"Come and listen to what the Lord your God says. Today you will know
that the living God is among you" (Joshua 3: 9–10).*

Although some contend that actions speak louder than words,
our souls are stirred and our hearts are warmed when "I love
you" is spoken. The special people in our lives affirm and
nurture us through verbal expressions of compassion, encour-
agement, and forgiveness. Can you recall kind or thoughtful
remarks from a beloved that was surely God's influence or
inspiration? A time God's goodness was expressed through
another? A time his voice of perseverance was in the cheer-
leading of a friend? Or when his whisper of hope came
through a reassuring partner?

We experience God in many different ways with our phys-
ical ears, but there are times when we are alone that we hear
him with the inner "ear" of our heart. There are moments our
hearts can hear gentle reminders of his promises through his
quiet whispers of love and affirmation when we invite him
into our silence.

Alone in Her Silence

Yesterday's dripping faucet echoes with the squeaking door,
And alone in her silence she hears the aging farm floor.

Old memories of the slamming screen, the telephone's ring,

And chattering children move her heart to wistfully wring.

Once, carefree laughter graced her with a peaceful poise,

And her husband's loving endearments muted the noise.

Now all alone in her silence, comforting thoughts she'll find,

As dear voices from her life drift fondly into mind.

Today's awareness of the Lord's love songs of sweet refrain

Are in the warm sunshine, restless wind, and gently falling rain.

With ears that barely discern, she boosts her inner volume to hear

Whispers of God's love and eternal promises drawing near.

"See how very much our heavenly Father loves us" (1 John 3:1).

Touching the Power of the Holy Spirit

Our sense of touch can evoke an awareness of God if, when we stroke a velvety rose petal or hold a firm apple, we will recall how they came to be. When we shape a snowball, carve a piece of wood, or work pastry dough, we are in touch with God's creations. As we work the soil to plant a flower, pluck it from the garden, or place it in a vase, we are touching God's beauty and a result of his love. Even as we touch a prickly cactus, rough pine tree bark, or sharp rose thorns, we are in a very real sense in touch with God, the Creator of all things.

What do you touch that brings God into focus for you? When you walk barefoot on the dampened seashore as the ocean sprays your face, do you feel God's touch? Do you contemplate God's powerful creativity as you filter a handful of sand between your fingertips or sculpt dampened sand into a recognizable form? If you pick up a seashell from the beach, do you marvel at the way it feels and ponder other gifts from the sea? When you place your hand in a bubbling brook to retrieve a smooth pebble worn by moving water, do you think of his power? When you pluck a wildflower persevering on your path, do you grow aware of his beauty in creation? Perhaps you marvel at the variety in God's creations when you walk through the forest and collect a bumpy pinecone, a crinkly leaf, or a delicate feather. Maybe his versatility occurs to you when you hold the fallen nut of an oak tree or the disturbed egg of a bird's nest.

Are you reminded of God when you touch an item or tool specific to your gifts or abilities such as a pen, a paintbrush, or a stethoscope? Perhaps when a chef measures ingredients to bake a cake or a carpenter hammers nails to build a house they ponder the source of their abilities through their sense of touch. When you wield a gardening tool, swing a golf club, or hold a book to participate in your hobby or pastime, are you reminded of your blessings? Maybe when you use tools for making scrap books, ride a bicycle, or swing a tennis racket you feel blessed to participate in leisurely activities.

I Feel God's Presence

I feel God's presence as I stroke my dog
And when I place a flower in a vase.
I feel God when I hold my grandson's hand
And in my granddaughter's ardent embrace.
I feel God's presence as I retire at night
And when I'm touched by my daughter's bright mind.
I feel God in the breaching of a massive whale
And when his spirit blesses the maligned.
I feel God's presence in my husband's strength
And when pride in my sons overflows my heart's rim.

I feel God's touch anchoring the center of my soul
And spreading a light that will never grow dim!

"And the Lord replied, 'I will personally go with you, Moses. I will give you rest—everything will be fine for you'" (Exodus 33:14).

One of the most profound avenues for experiencing the presence of God through our sense of touch is when we touch one another. We can be reminded of our Creator whether bathing our baby, rocking our grandchild, or hugging our parents. Holding hands with a beloved, kissing a child's cheek, or patting a teenager's back is connecting with the Holy Spirit. When we cradle an infant, hug a friend, or embrace our spouse, we are experiencing God's love. We are touching God whether we touch a baby's young, silky body or a grandfather's aging, wrinkled hand. Our hearts and souls are cradled by a divine love when we are hugged with warmth and sincerity. God's goodness touches us through the comforting hand, and his kindness touches us in a wordless embrace.

His Touch

His touch enters our hearts through a sunray
And soothes as we bask in a gentle breeze.
His touch is in the miracle of a newborn baby
And in the kindness of a friend hugging to ease.
His touch is in the arms of a caring grandfather
And in daddy's hand smoothing his child's hair.
His touch cradles our souls in the moonlight,
Inspiring a bridge of trust in a friendship fair.

His touch is in the message from his Holy Word
And in the silken petals of a delicate rosebud.
His touch is in the bravery of a soldier
And in the pool of his sacrificed blood.

*"Honor and majesty surround him; strength and beauty are in his
sanctuary. O nations of the world, recognize the Lord; recognize that
the Lord is glorious and strong. Give to the Lord the glory he deserves!"
(Psalm 96:6–8).*

Tasting the Fruit of God's Love

We can be attuned to our Creator through his edible creations. God not only advances life, but also enhances life through our taste buds, whether we are enjoying a stew combining vegetables from the garden, a juicy strawberry from the vine, or a chocolate crème delight, which originated in the pod of a tree. We are grateful for the food that nourishes our bodies, and we enjoy the wonderful flavors and enticing textures of food, as well. Eating is a pleasurable experience. Each of us could create a list of edibles that not only provide sustenance but tickle our taste buds with sheer delight. Topping my list is sweet, sweet ice cream! What about you? What about your taste buds? What surfaces to remind you that God is the Creator of all things edible?

Incredible Edibles

Gracing our lives with incredible edibles,
Providing purely palatable pleasures,
Our Creator blesses and nourishes our bodies
With his taste-filled, delectable treasures!

"Everything we have has come from you!" (1 Chronicles 29:14).

God not only feeds our bodies, but he also feeds our hungry hearts and nourishes our barren souls. As we draw near to God and invite his forgiveness, his infinite, unconditional love feeds our hearts with hope. His kind, benevolent mercy fills our souls with joy. His beautiful, generous grace blesses our lives with peace. God's soul food, his manna from heaven, is vital to contentment. Fulfillment in life can be ours regardless of our circumstances as we invite and receive God's sustaining bread of life.

Bread of Life

Our Creator's divine redeeming plan
Of extending mercy from his Kingdom above
Sheds his light of grace to each soul
And feeds every heart with unconditional love.
Jesus our Lord, who is the bread of life,
Supplies our hearts with his spirit of hope.
He infuses our souls with amazing peace
And rekindles joy from his generous scope.
Our Lord, with his kind, forgiving spirit,
Offers our hearts the bread of life to interlace
With his sweet and powerful sovereign love,
Soothing our souls beyond his earthly grace.

*"Jesus replied, 'I am the bread of life. No one who comes to me will ever
be hungry again. Those who believe in me will never thirst'"
(John 6:35).*

Smelling the Labor of the Lord

There are aromas familiar to all of us, and there are those unique to our individual life experiences. Scents can evoke memories that move us into a sense of God's current involvement in our lives.

Aromatic Memories

When thoughts determine to lazily drift,
Bringing to my heart a warm pungent lift,
I return to my yesterdays and let memories flow,
Recalling aromas my heart'll forever know.
Reliving the warm scent of a freshly baked pie
Causes contentment to waft to a special high.
And the freshly baked cookies I smell even now
Trigger reasons my mama should come take a bow.
The newly mown hay cut by Daddy's plough
Emitted an odor that stayed with me somehow.
And each spring the smell of freshly falling rain
Creates images of the crops of golden grain.
The strong aroma of the old-fashioned evergreen tree
Stirs warm comforting memories deep within me.
My daddy cut a cedar every Christmas on the farm,
And Mama helped adorn with a fun, festive charm.

"Since everything God created is good, we should not reject any of it. We may receive it gladly, with thankful hearts. For we know it is made holy by the word of God and prayer" (1 *Timothy* 4:4–5).

Our minds could wander endlessly to include all of the ways God enters our souls through our sense of smell. We receive his creative genius as we sniff the perfume of the flower, whiff the cinnamon in pastry, or smell rainfall in the air. The aroma of newly mown grass or the fragrance of a lilac bush may encourage us to reflect on the gift of family. The scent of baby powder may remind us that a baby is a gift from God.

Can you realize God's handiwork in your list of aromas? Do special scents evoke memories of a specific beloved? Perhaps the aroma of pot roast or a certain perfume reminds you of Mama, while the smell of popcorn or shaving cream reminds you of Daddy. Does the smell of furniture polish bring Grandma to mind? Does a specific soap scent remind you of Grandpa? Perhaps the scent of chocolate returns youthful memories of sharing your mother's pecan fudge with siblings. Maybe it evokes your reflections of receiving a box of chocolates on Valentine's Day from someone special. Or the scent of chocolate may remind you of relaxing over hot cocoa with your brother or sister after creating a snowman or making angel wings in the snow. What about the smell of hotdogs, mustard, or pickles? Do these aromas recall blessings of good family times, fun movie dates, or memorable church picnics that were orchestrated by God?

What do we mean when we remark that we smell a touch of autumn in the air? Do we smell summer growth transitioning into autumn as the breezes blow across the fallen leaves? When we comment that it feels like spring is in the air, are we implying that an aroma is moving life from winter rest into spring revival? Do we smell something different when summer warms and nurtures new life? Do we "smell" a correlation of God's changing seasons with our own changing lives? Are we realizing it is part of God's plan to provide us with times for rebirth, periods for productivity, seasons for transition, and spells for rest, just as he does for the plant life? Whatever the answers may be, we all have our own file of scents that recall various aspects of our lives. We each have aromas in our minds that unfold our past and enhance our current awareness of God. Many of them trigger our desires to participate in God's goodness. They help us relate to past experiences or emotions that bear the mark of his kindness.

Drawing Near God through Our Senses

Several years ago, on a beautiful autumn day in the mountains, persuasive friends indirectly blessed my life with an invitation to go hiking. I walked that day with my husband and friends in some of God's most magnificent mountains. Surrounded by incredible beauty, I could smell the cool, clean mountain air and the distinct aroma of cedar and pine. I heard God in the chirping birds, skittering chipmunks, and distant elk. I savored a treasured snack and touched the fallen snow. God waited at the pinnacle with a glacier lake that mirrored a reflection of spectacular beauty. Like a work of art, the surrounding scenery floated serenely on the water. I experienced God with all of my senses that day in the mountains. I knew he was there, for I could feel his presence as his marvelous creations caught my breath and filled me with joy.

My mountaintop experience marked a pronounced awakening to the Holy Spirit through all of my senses. Slowly, I began to grow more and more aware of the prevalence of God's presence.

God is Everywhere

God glows in each ray of the golden sun.

He's gathered in the shiny raindrops of a leaf

He's sprinkled amidst the field of yellow daisies
And dwells in a heart bearing disbelief.
God is in the pastel colors that dress the sky.
He walks in the rhythm of an elderly pace.
He's in snowflake sprinkles of pure delight
And in a little child's innocent face.
God is in lowly lambs of lush green valleys.
He's in a mother's tender touch on a feverish brow.
He's in playful dolphins slicing the ocean blue
And in the noisy blue jay jeering on a bough.
God is in the fresh aroma of a cool spring rain.
He's in the gift of chocolate, velvety and sweet.
He's in the beauty of a colorful, perfumed flower,
And his boundless love makes our lives complete.

"Listen, and I will tell you where to get food that is good for the soul!"
(Isaiah 55:2).

I felt blessed to be in the company of my beloved spouse and two longtime friends on that lovely day in the mountains. The uplifting mountain experience remained with me and heightened my desire to learn more about God. Gradually, I grew increasingly aware of God as I encountered him in others and discovered him in the world of nature.

You Were Waiting

I heard you this morning, dear Lord,
In the sweet sparrow, fluttering its wings.

I heard you in the rat-a-tat-tat of the woodpecker
And in a bright red cardinal perched high to sing.
I sensed your loyalty in my beloved dog
And I felt your gentle kiss graze my cheek.
Your love whispered my name in a breeze,
And the subtlety inspired me to seek.
I saw you in the whirling shadows of the sun
And smelled your essence in the morning air.
Your sweet serenity encouraged my tears
In my beautiful haven of devoted care.
You were watching for me in my garden
With warm sunrays to thaw my frozen heart.
You were waiting in the melodious songbirds,
Singing sweet salutations of love to impart.

"Surely your goodness and unfailing love will pursue me all the days of my life, and I will live in the house of the Lord forever" (Psalm 23:6).

God desires that we realize he is everywhere. He wants us to grow aware of his beauty, wisdom, and power. He wants us to know he prevails as the creator of the universe. Every day there are many ways in which we are drawn into God's presence through our senses of seeing, hearing, touching, tasting, and smelling. As we gradually realize that God is everywhere, we grow more and more adept at recognizing and appreciating him. Our awareness of the presence of God increases as we begin to see him, not only in the obvious or expected but in the subtle, the hidden, and the unimaginable.

The Sunflower

The sunflower turns a confident golden face
Toward the commanding sun of another day,
Quietly absorbing its nurturing power,
Following innately until night has its way.
The sunflower tracks the steady sunrays,
Faithfully trusting in God and his Kingdom,
Moving in unison with the governing sun,
Devotedly shifting with uncanny wisdom.
When we imitate the colorful sunflower,
Wisely following every day God's guiding light,
We silently express the color of our faithfulness
As he leads us with love, nurturing and right.
When we trust in God to lead us every hour,
Telling us when to go, when to stop, and when to rest,
Always inviting him to chart our daily paths,
He feeds our hearts to continue our earthly quest.

*"You chart the path ahead of me and tell me where to stop and rest.
Every moment you know where I am" (Psalm 139:3).*

We can sense God in mild and ordinary ways or in bold and uncommon ways. Sometimes his presence is as obvious as the brilliant sunset and sometimes as subtle as a simple act of kindness. We can readily recognize God in a powerful sunrise, but can we see the capacity of God's love in the act of forgiveness? We can easily feel God in a lovely garden, but can we experience him in the art of acceptance? We see God's profound touch in heaven's galaxy, but do we feel him as we encounter the downtrodden?

God is everywhere. We often fail to focus on God. Sometimes we take his presence for granted in simple and ordinary things and overlook him in the majestic and miraculous. We can experience God through all of our senses, but in reality we needn't look far, for we house the ultimate source of encountering and experiencing God. We carry the Holy Spirit within our hearts. We can choose to acknowledge and invite God's presence. We can draw into the infinite presence of God and feel him draw close to us. He awaits.

The Infinite Presence of God

God's *majesty* is in the towering mountains,

And his *power* reigns over the turbulent seas.

His *comfort* rests in the soul struggling with grief,

And his *perseverance* holds the hand of the blind.

His *creativity* is revealed in an exquisite butterfly,

And his *gentleness* is in a mother's tender hand.

His *calm* is in the mind, relaxed and stress-free,

And his *protection* flies with the birds of the air.

His *goodness* resides in the nurturing caregiver,

And his *kindness* is in the welcome raindrops.

His *generosity* is in the provisions for survival,

And his *tenderness* is in a fragile newborn.

His *patience* is in the father teaching his child,

And his *magic* is in the delicate snowflake.

His *faithfulness* rides in the endless ocean waves,

And his *hope* can be seen thriving in the ill.

His *strength* is presented in the powerful wind,

And his *beauty* rests in grandmother's smile.

His *mercy* reigns in the forgiving spirit,

And his *loyalty* lies within the heart of a dog.

His *restoration* blesses a soul soaring free,

And his *perfection* prevails in the fragrant rose.

His *courage* lies within the determined explorer,

And his *trust* is in the heart of an innocent child.

His *peace* ambles in the shepherded lamb,

And his *joy* is in the lilt of the songbird.

His *wisdom* is in a grandfather's guidance,

And his *love* dwells in the heart of you and me.

"I love your sanctuary, Lord, the place where your glory shines"
(Psalm 26:8).

Awakening to God's Presence through People

The indwelling Holy Spirit produces Christian virtues in the life of the believer. In the New Testament the Apostle Paul informs us, "But when the Holy Spirit controls our lives, he will produce this kind of fruit in us: love, joy, peace, patience, kindness, goodness, faithfulness, gentleness, and self-control" (Galatians 5:22–23). Our acts of mercy and grace are manifestations of the Holy Spirit dwelling within us. We plant a positive seed about God when we extend his unconditional love. Potent seeds are planted about the character of our Creator when our lives reflect his righteousness.

We perceive God in one another with the inner vision of our hearts and the internal ears of our souls. When we listen artfully and encourage compassionately with kindness and goodness, we reflect God's spirit. His hope is in a joyful heart. His peace is in a gentle soul. God is seen in strong and courageous people who persevere with hope and joy through trials. He is found in those who find peace in the clamor and upheaval of life. We can awaken to God's presence through a life that reflects God's light.

I experienced God through others. As I ponder my stirring awareness of God, I recognize how important the unconditional love of my family and friends was to my spiritual growth. Those who expressed God's gentleness, goodness, and kindness were an inspiration to me. During a difficult time in my life I received the gifts of hope and encouragement from specific friends who were willing to listen patiently and compassionately to me. An aunt who was thoughtful, gentle, and caring graced my life. The love and loyalty of my parents and sisters were blessings on my walk of faith. The Holy Spirit was evident in my beloved husband's quiet inner strength. His life has reflected the Christian virtues of love, kindness, goodness, faithfulness, and patience. My life has been enriched by the love my dear children and I have shared. Their good and gentle souls were a reminder of God's divinity that dwells within us all.

Others nurtured the seeds planted in my soul about God. Special women in my life endured difficult or tragic circumstances. I was importantly influenced spiritually by the courage and strength of my sister-in-law as she continued to seek hope and retain joy during the strain and sorrow of her husband's terminal illness. My faith was further ignited by the quiet inner strength of a dear friend who sought peace during the tragic loss of her beloved son. Her ability to persevere through her sorrow and smile through her tears was encouraging to my own quest for peace. Additionally, certain other dear friends were wonderful examples of hope and perseverance as they continued to laugh and expound upon the glory of knowing God even as family members struggled with alcohol and drug abuse. All of these women were an inspiration in my life and impacted my faith journey as I observed their reliance on the Lord. They influenced my ability to be joyful during difficult times. They taught me to remain hopeful during discouraging situations. Many times I was reminded of God's character and his goodness as I watched these women find strength in him. I pondered the inspiration they surely were to others as well.

The seeds planted in me about God when I was a child growing up in the country were nurtured over the years in many places, including the church. My walk of faith was enriched in small faith sharing groups, Sunday school classes, and Bible classes. Every year the Christmas story of Jesus' birth reminded me of the blessings of peace and joy that come to us through God's powerful love. I felt the hope for eternal life through the Easter story of Christ's Crucifixion and Resurrection. Time and time again I was stirred to awaken to God's presence through the welcoming spirit of the congregation, the inspiring messages from the pulpit, and the talent within the music ministry.

A Singer

A gifted singer awakens my soul

As lilting, golden strains enfold.

Important inspirational lyrics

Bless me with glorious riches untold!

My spirit is aroused by the ultimate Source

As I receive the gift of the singer's voice.

I marvel at the God-given talent,

And with gratitude I inwardly rejoice.

> *"God has given each of us the ability to do certain things well"*
> *(Romans 12:6).*

Perhaps you, too, have been moved by a heart-stopping voice or touched by a breathtaking dancer. God bestows talents, gifts, and abilities on each of us to glorify his name. We recognize God in the woman with an ability to teach, the boy born to be in sales, or the man destined to become an accomplished author. What about the nurse's endurance, the hairdresser's skills, or the accountant's accuracy? Isn't the conscientious homemaker, the persistent choir director, or the diligent construction worker also utilizing his or her gifts from God? What of those with the ability to organize, communicate, or lead? And what about those who quietly extend mercy, give graciously, or love well? Can you see God within your own talents, gifts, or abilities?

We each see and feel God differently as our individual personalities and experiences form our perceptions. We receive God's gift of imagination through a spellbinding novel or an inspiring movie. We are experiencing God through a talented actor, an incredible dancer, or a gifted singer. His power of inspiration can be seen in a remarkable oil painting or an outstanding photograph. His beauty comes through the eye of a glass blower or the soul of a musician. God's generosity is in a carefully sculpted statue, a painstakingly stitched quilt, or a perfectly balanced floral arrangement. His power is realized in the sweeping wheat fields and the blooming fruit orchards. His love is experienced through a mother's pecan pie, a grandmother's embroidery, or a friend's garden. God's love is expressed through a kind note, a thoughtful phone call, or a considerate inquiry. We gradually grow adept at recognizing God's presence in others and ourselves as we see him at work in countless ways.

Maybe you have felt the Holy Spirit moving through the profound words of a minister or the compassionate patience of a teacher. Quite likely you have experienced the smiling heart of a woman seated next to you in a waiting room or the generous soul of a man at your place of work. Perhaps you have felt God reaching out to help you through a neighbor or Jesus has cradled you through the comfort of a caregiver. Has a random act of kindness drawn you into the presence of God? Have you felt blessed by a saving spirit when a friend, spouse, or stranger extended forgiveness? Has the receipt of unconditional love filled you with joy? Has your confidence to persevere come from the encouragement of a friend or loved one? Do you have a friend, a child, or a sibling with a gift for listening? To whom do you extend patience and self-control? Can others sense God's peace abiding in you? Can his joy be seen in your smile and his gentleness in your speech? Can his hope be heard in your words?

God is everywhere. We see the Holy Spirit in those who are blessed with an abiding faith and trust in God. We also see him in those seeking answers, bearing grief, or struggling to believe. We can feel the heart of our Redeemer at home, at work, or at church. We can find him in people at the mall or the supermarket. We can experience him through our parents, spouses, children, and siblings. He can come to us through friends and strangers.

We can experience God through the strength, wisdom, and bravery of others. We can feel God's inspiration when we reflect on a persevering researcher, a dedicated world leader, or an ingenious inventor. Our Creator can come to mind as we ponder the marvels of an architect, the ability of a mechanic, or the skills of an engineer. Surely the source of strength and courage for the pioneer, farmer, or explorer is from the Unseen.

The Unseen

How did immigrants derive the courage
To go on when life was turned upside down?

Did determination come from the Unseen?

And hope from a heavenly crown?

Did Divinity dwell in the bold and brave?

And within the fortitude of ancestral strains?

When pioneers forged trails in new territories,

Were they in rhythm with the Unseen of the plains?

Ponder the perseverance of a great explorer,

Encouraged by the Unseen to be brave,

And marvel as you reflect on the tenacity

Of those who dwelled in an ancient cave.

Envision a mighty invisible Power

Within those recognizing the land's worth,

And wonder at the endurance of the farmer

Planting, tending, and harvesting the earth.

"From the time the world was created, people have seen the earth and sky and all that God made. They can clearly see his invisible qualities— his eternal power and divine nature" (Romans 1:20).

Sometimes we see God in others in subtle ways, and sometimes we see him in bold ways. Some of the ways we perceive God are minor, and some are profound. Some are common, and some are rare. A yellow plumeria flower tucked into the raven hair of an island woman as she moves fluidly to melodious lyrics is more than a lovely vision to behold.

Soul Stirring

Soulfully a smile spread over her face
As slowly she moved with the song.
And serenely her arms kept perfect pace
While her feet moved fluidly along.
Nestling a yellow plumeria in her raven hair,
Sharing pure peace from the Spirit that calms,
Sweetly she moved with concentrated care
Against an orange sunset, framed by black palms.
Arousing my thoughts to reverent ascent,
Her graceful rhythm and gentle sway,
Amid melodious music of soulful content,
Conveyed God's "aloha" the Hawaiian way!

"A time to cry and a time to laugh.
A time to grieve and a time to dance" (Ecclesiastes 3:4).

We easily recognize God in some people, while in others it is more difficult. It is harder for us to believe the Holy Spirit dwells within the criminal or the enemy. Many of us simply turn away from a life that is foreign to us. We have a tendency to shut down when we do not understand someone. We are likely to dismiss them if they do not fit our preconceived notions of what is right, worthy, or good. Our Creator challenges us to follow the example of Jesus to embrace the forgotten, the rejected, and the lonely. He asks us to love those who are despised or misunderstood. Our Redeemer asks us to love the unlovable. He desires that we love unconditionally, as he loves us, regardless of our shortcomings or differences.

God works boldly through the special gifts of specific people to increase awareness of his fairness, faithfulness, and unconditional love. He sends unique people to help us feel his powerful presence. Mother Teresa was born Agnes Gonxha Bojaxhiu in 1910 in Skoplje, Yugoslavia, which is now Macedonia. She was a humanitarian and missionary who dedicated her life to serving the hungry, the poor, and the downtrodden. Often referred to as a living saint, Mother Teresa was once introduced to a group of people as the most powerful woman in the world. Her profound service to those in need was known across the nations. Her strong love for others grew out of her deep love for Jesus Christ. The Holy Spirit instilled compassion within her. She believed God creates us out of love and wants to be in relationship with us. She believed strongly that we are created to return his love.[1]

Mother Teresa, with abundant compassion, wise understanding, and abiding faith, made a profound difference to countless people. She lived by her words and was led by God's empowering love to embrace even the lowliest of humanity. Mother Teresa believed it requires staying in the presence of God and listening as well as speaking to him in a consistent prayer life to live our lives from the foundation of his unconditional love. She believed willingness to be of service to others would grow from our love for God. She held a strong belief in the power of prayer to bind people together in his love. The Holy Scripture inspired Mother Teresa's core message that God is love.

The Core Message

The core message from God's Kingdom,

The greatest gift we'll ever know,

Is his resurrecting, infinite love

He so kindly and generously bestows.

God's goal is to marry faith, hope, and love

Within the inner chambers of our hearts.

His core message of endless love,

He generously and faithfully imparts!

*"There are three things that will endure—faith, hope and love—and the greatest of these is love" (*1 Corinthians 13:13*).*

We are called to follow the example of unconditional love Jesus displayed while here on earth. The power of God's absolute love is evident when it is offered without judgment, condemnation, or intolerance. We experience God through the important gifts of people like Mother Teresa who are known throughout the world for spreading God's light with profound compassion. Like a moth attracted to a flame, people are attracted to the light of God's love that shines through others. I was a moth one Sunday, a stranger drawn into deep reflection of the Holy Spirit in a sanctuary full of flexible minds and peaceful souls. I saw God's spirit in the living compassion of people with open arms, sincere smiles, and accepting hearts.

Accepting Hearts

Sweet feelings were there, floating in the air
Of humility, gratitude, and unconditional love.
It was on the smile of a face extending grace
As it descended from the Savior above.
Celebrating the gift of a loving relationship,
Appreciating uniqueness, yours and mine,
Accepting each identity, color, and race,
We worshipped as one, the Holy Spirit divine!

> *"Anyone who says, 'I am in the light' but rejects
> another Christian is still in darkness" (1 John 2:9).*

Studying the life of Christ teaches us that his love is all-inclusive. We are called to follow his example of love to include everyone, regardless of gender, color, race, sexual orientation, or status in life. Stepping out of our "box" to love and serve without exclusion is difficult. It requires extra courage to leave our comfort zones. He will help us as we invite his abiding influence. He will inspire goodness in our hearts that will reflect his light strongly enough to encourage others to follow him. God will empower us to be a divine reflection of his love as exemplified by Mother Teresa.

A Divine Reflection

Her kind heart was like an extraordinary flower
Whose deep roots were fed by God's loving care.
She was a fragrant rosebud of incredible beauty

With unique silky petals, tolerant and fair.

Her wise spirit was like a gentle summer breeze

Rippling the clinging leaves of a towering tree.

And her strength to persevere through a storm

Was given her by a love that sets the soul free.

She was the ever faithful, brightly rising sun

Shining her belief with an enchanting warm glow.

And the hope in her heart on a mountaintop high

Brought peace to her soul in the valley below.

She was a divine reflection of God's amazing grace,

Humbly sharing the beauty of his wondrous love.

She quietly emitted a beacon of his powerful light

And helped guide his sheep to his throne above.

"You are the light of the world—like a city on a mountain, glowing in the night for all to see. Don't hide your light under a basket! Instead, put it on a stand and let it shine for all. In the same way, let your good deeds shine out for all to see, so that everyone will praise your heavenly Father" (Matthew 5:14–16).

Mother Teresa plugged into the power of God and received his energy and love. He reflected his light through her to guide and assist innumerable people. She personified the grace of his divine presence with humility and great honor. Empowered by our Creator, she spent her life making God's light visible to the world. God desires that we seek a higher level of awareness of him and his unconditional love, which was so beautifully mirrored in the life of Mother Teresa. He asks us to follow her example of mercy and compassion. He encourages us to emulate her dedication to follow him with faith and trust. We are called to recognize God as love and recognize the power in his love.

The Power in His Love

God's love is more *precious* than a baby's sweet smile
And more *majestic* than the highest mountain peak.
God's love is *stronger* than winds of hurricane force
And more *reliable* than the sea's endless ebb and flow.
God's love is more *restorative* than winter's retreat
And more *anointing* than our life's greatest achievement.
God's love is more *infinite* than heaven's ceiling
And *brighter* than the sunshine reigning in the sky.
God's love is more *satisfying* than worldly rewards
And more *validating* than all earthen treasures.
God's love is more *profound* than any to receive,
And his *powerful* love inspires us to flourish and mature.

"Surely your goodness and unfailing love will pursue me all the days of my life, and I will live in the house of the Lord forever" (Psalm 23:6).

Awakening to God's Presence through Our Trials

Am I the only one, Lord, who is detained by dark clouds, laden with the strong winds of fear? Am I the only pilgrim who trembles from stormy challenges or turbulent guilt? Am I the only Christian who struggles to focus spiritually when treading troubled water? In the early stages of my pilgrimage, these were questions I asked God as I struggled with how to journey with him. I felt I was the only one who slipped into anxiety-filled ditches or tripped over piles of doubt. Roadblocks of confusion popped up to throw me off track for hours, if not days at a time. I often felt alone in my trials and did not understand what good could ever come from them or how they could deepen my faith. How could difficulties more closely align me with God? How could hardships draw me into his powerful presence? I sought understanding about the correlation between going through trials and growing with the Lord.

We long for a miraculous rescue from our trials. We want solutions to our problems and answers to our questions. We yearn for comfort when we hurt and encouragement when we are dejected. We wish anxiety, doubt, and fear were strangers to our lives. It is not unusual for our hope to dissipate, our joy to drift away, and our peace to disappear when we are burdened by trials. We long for a light to guide us through our dark times and expose our joy. At our low ebb we crave hallowed hope and perfect peace to center us in our tilted world.

When we turn to God with childlike faith and trust, he will help us. He will respond to our needs with his "manna from heaven" as a loving parent does to his or her child. God loves us so much that when we invite his help, he will empower us with the courage and strength to persevere. When we flounder in strong currents of trouble, he will be our anchor. When we are adrift in a sea of sorrow, like a faithful lighthouse he will guide us to the security of the shore. He will rescue us from the valley of darkness and return us to the light of hope. Our relationship with God deepens as we find peace in his presence.

Peace

Even though our dreams may crumble

When devastating doubts derail

And our hopes drown in a sea of sorrow

As guilt or shame tries to impale ...

Even though stress alters our focus

And hopelessness hovers like a dark cloud,

Jesus Christ will deliver incredible peace

And remove turmoil seeking to enshroud.

Even though anxieties relentlessly return,

Like ocean waves pounding the shore,
And tentacles of dark fear try to spread,
God's soothing peace will guard and restore.

"If you do this, you will experience God's peace, which is far more wonderful than the human mind can understand. His peace will guard your hearts and minds as you live in Christ Jesus" (Philippians 4:7).

Our earthly relationships are enriched as we share our lives. We connect with a peaceful, open mind and a joyful, grateful heart. We are drawn to the hope in those with a compassionate and forgiving spirit. Our spirits meld as love and loyalty grow through sharing and caring. Even more powerfully, our relationship with our heavenly Father flourishes as we share our lives with him. Our connection to God is strengthened when we focus on his presence during ordinary days, as well as during remarkable ones. Even more so our bond with God tightens during the trial of sadness or difficulty as we experience his presence in the midst of them. Our friendship with our Creator is nourished as we receive his consistent, supportive love. It is a beautiful blessing to move through trials with our Redeemer and grow stronger, lighter, and wiser from the intimacy that develops with him as we draw near him and feel him draw near to us.

Our lives are like a tapestry wherein God's bright threads of love and forgiveness are woven over our threads of transgressions. Encouraging threads of reassurance replace our threads of oppression, fear, and doubt. Sweet strands of joy rise above our sour strands of resentment, guilt, or regret. His golden filaments of hope cast a beautiful glow over our threads of discouragement. His silken threads of peace overshadow our threads of turmoil. He shines his silver strands of grace over our strands of sorrow. God's strength contrasting with our weakness produces a unique and profound weaving. Our soul tapestries grow stronger, lovelier, and worthier as we follow God humbly with love, gratitude, and praise.

God's work in our tapestries does not eliminate our trials or exempt us from further sadness or hardships, but our burdens grow lighter in his presence. Our troubles lose their power to control us as we acknowledge his faithfulness. Disappointment and despair begin to fade as we invite the light in his encouragement to weave a contrast with our darkness. In God's presence the unbearable feels bearable and the impossible feels possible. When we intertwine our lives with God and trust him to carry our burdens, just as a little child does with his or her parent, we are rewarded with the courage to persevere. It will not necessarily be easy. It may at times feel impossible, but when we adhere to God and revere him through everything, over time our tapestries will be enhanced.

Adhere and Revere

He infiltrates our storm clouds with rays of hope
And he whispers our name in the quake of despair.
He showers sweet peace to dissolve our tears
And lends reassurance with interceding prayer.
The Songbird of Heaven sings of renewal
And lulls shadows of sorrow from our souls.
He buoys our spirits with uplifting joy
And offers his love to uphold and console.
The incredible light of his love sparks belief,
And his amazing grace ignites us to persevere.
The mercy in our Lord's gentle whisper
Encourages us to adhere and revere!

"And after the earthquake there was a fire, but the Lord was not in the
fire. And after the fire there was the sound of a gentle whisper"
(1 Kings 19:12).

Trials have the power to shake our faith. We struggle to stay centered in God when our lives have been turned upside down. When illness, loss, or grief strikes, it can obscure our vision of God and his power to help. During these times doubt and fear can snake throughout our being and take control of our lives. We may even feel abandoned by God when bad things happen to us. We need help to keep our eyes on the source of hope. We need help to stay focused on God and his power to help us in our trials.

Choosing to walk closely with God during hardships will help us begin to understand the width of his mercy and the height of his grace. We will experience the depth of God's love when we focus on him during our trials. Our friendship with the Lord deepens and results in profound spiritual growth when our trials draw us close to him. Thus, trials are blessings in disguise when they lead us to God's empowering love. God's greatness and goodness come as we draw near to him and feel him draw near to us with a ray of hope, a sparkle of joy, and a glimmer of peace—a silver lining for our dark cloud.

Silver Lining

Sunshine flees my world, graying my soul

When sadness shouts out my name.

I wonder what good can come from pain

When harsh winds extinguish my flames.

I can scarcely imagine the storm-laden clouds,

Delivering trouble-filled showers,

Could be sporting a sweet silver lining

As I live through pain-filled hours.

But when I hear God whispering my name,

A faint feeling of peace comes into view,

And the elusive hope that felt forever gone

Returns to my thoughts to lift me anew.

When God kindly whispers, "My dear child,

Let my embrace return a smile to your face,

And let my colorful rainbow brighten your soul,"

I begin to feel his glorious hope enter my space.

Yes, God saves me from the ashes,

And he lifts me from a fall.

He carries me over the chasm

And hears the anguish in my call.

Out of the embers of burning sadness,

God furnishes his living waters to sustain.

He offers hallowed hope to save and enrich

And his gift of joy becomes my gain.

With his loving, merciful countenance

God penetrates the darkness with his light

And reveals hope in some miraculous hour

While shining his compassion on my plight.

Yes, a silver lining appears through the darkness

As God's light of hope begins to empower.

Mercifully he reveals a sliver of silver peace

That glows brighter and brighter by the hour!

*"And we know that God causes everything to work together for the good of those who love God and are called according to his purpose for them"
(Romans 8:28).*

Discovering God's love is the ultimate gift in life. The experience of awakening to God's presence and drawing close to him may be quiet and unremarkable, or it may be quite memorable and profound. Some of us grow aware of God gradually over a long period of time, while others of us feel his powerful presence rather suddenly during a special, single experience. Many of us awaken to God's presence during one of our trials. Surely this experience is unique for each of us. Regardless of the circumstances or timing of our enlightenment about God, when we discover his powerful presence and remain with him day after day through good times and bad times and the ordinary times in between, we eventually realize that no other source offers us more.

No Other Source

No other source offers more love

Or replaces anxiety with peace

And as we remain focused upon him,

The chains of fear, he will gladly release.

No other source can offer hallowed hope

When discouragement is slow to subside

Or lift our spirits with rare jubilant joy

When despair determines to abide.

No other source better restores vision

When our choices leave us too blind to see

Or sheds a light that shines any brighter

When we seek a new way on bended knee.

No other source offers more solace

When our day grows sad and long,

Or sends a sweeter message of absolution

When we err or are regrettably wrong.

No other source could ever sustain more

Or with our souls more beautifully blend.

Worthy of great praise, we revere the Lord,

Our Comforter, Protector, and Friend!

"Great is the Lord! He is most worthy of praise!
He is to be revered above all the gods" (Psalm 96:4).

The love we find in God's presence during our trials gives us the strength and courage to persevere. The hope we find in his reassurance during upheaval brings about an unexplainable peace. Hearing God's whisper of encouragement through our tears fills our hearts with gratitude and floods our souls with unexpected joy. These beautiful blessings come to us as we rely on God during our time of need. It is wonderful to feel God's love and receive his blessings every day, but during times of trouble and heartache it becomes profound.

When we discover confident expectation for our salvation comes from the powerful Spirit of love that lives within our hearts, it is a reason for rejoicing. When our hardships draw us to a pinnacle in our relationship with God, we will discover there is no greater relationship, no greater friend, and no greater counselor than our Lord.

"We can rejoice, too, when we run into problems or trials, for we know that they are good for us—they help us learn to endure. And endurance develops strength of character in us, and character strengthens our confident expectation of salvation. And this expectation will not disappoint us. For we know how dearly God loves us, because he has given us the Holy Spirit to fill our hearts with his love" (Romans 5:3–5).

Choosing to Journey in the Presence of an Extraordinary Guide

How can we feel God's presence? It really isn't difficult once we awaken and choose to draw close to him. We do not have to be on a retreat in Tibet or on a vacation in Belize to experience God. We do not have to ride a powerful ocean wave or scale a mighty mountain to know God's presence. We do not have to win a Nobel Prize or write a famous novel to be blessed by him. Nor do we have to win someone's approval or earn a trophy for best citizen to feel God draw near to us. We only need to trust that God is near, choose to focus on him, and practice being in his presence every day. We only need to remember he is always with us wherever we are and in whatever we do. We can be still and know who he is.

"Be silent, and know that I am God." (Psalm 46:10).

We can choose to walk through life with a Guide who promises moments of surprising joy during our trials. We can follow a Guide who grants times of unexplainable peace amidst confusion. We can rely on a Guide who leads us to days of unbelievable hope through our difficult circumstances. Our faithfulness to follow this extraordinary Guide will lead us to a level of contentment that need not remain elusive or unobtainable.

Although it will not be easy, we can trust the journey will be worthwhile, as the Guide will ultimately lead us to a life victorious on earth and a glorious one beyond. We will need to believe he is a Guide whose credentials will surpass our expectations. We will need faith to journey with a Guide we cannot see. We will not know the length of our journey or the daily itinerary. We must accept that there will be mysteries surrounding the Guide, the journey, and the final destination. When we grow weary or discouraged, we can trust he will give us rest. When we become anxious or fearful, we can believe that as we remain faithful and patient he will eventually lead us to peace, one day at a time. We can rely on his wisdom to teach us to retain joy through our hardships. We can trust his power to anchor us during our storms. We can believe he will help us appreciate mundane days and learn to bypass the tedious with grace.

We must remember that as we are unable to see our Guide, we must remain connected to him through prayer to hear his whispers of reassurance. We must stay tuned with the inner ear of our hearts to hear his sweet affirmations of hope. We will need to heed the holy Word of his Guidebook that has sustained followers throughout time. He will guide us in his way and in his timing as we enter his presence, invite his assistance, and learn to wait patiently for his direction.

"Be still in the presence of the Lord, and wait patiently for him to act"
(Psalm 37:7).

It will require extra strength to remain dedicated to our Guide when we become overwhelmed by our commitment. When we become discouraged we can recall the testimonies of fellow pilgrims about God's willingness and incredible ability to help them at their point of need. We can remember God has been proclaimed through the ages to excel as teacher, comforter, and guide. We can seek his wisdom to help us make good decisions for our journeys. Even though we cannot see our Guide, we can focus on our perception of him and trust him on a level beyond our understanding.

Beyond Understanding

Beyond understanding the sea reclaims the land at whim,
And faithfully the waves recede to the sea's rim.
The mountains erupt and spout ribbons of fire
And caress cushions floating in the heavenly empire.
The incredible sun moves in rhythm with the earth,
And sends forth an energy of incalculable worth!
Beyond understanding a heart is freed by forgiving grace
And a loving power inspires an understanding embrace.
Merciful acceptance infuses a weak spirit with power,
And the beauty of compassion stimulates a soul to flower.
Kindness floods hope into the heart of the rejected and poor,
And the gift of encouragement sparks the spirit to endure.
Beyond understanding, a holy, sovereign power
Displays righteous love hour after hour.
An invisible, yet brilliantly glowing face,
Mercifully grants forgiveness with amazing grace.

A Supreme Being, above any authority of the land
Begins a gradual transformation with an outstretched hand.

*"Now he is far above any ruler or authority or power or leader or any-
thing else in this world or in the world to come" (Ephesians 1:21).*

How will we travel each day? Will we cruise joyfully in
beautiful surroundings on a luxurious ocean liner or traverse
dejectedly through treacherous territory on weary feet? Will
we soar excitedly through peaceful air or rumble monoto-
nously through barren land? Will we stroll confidently down
a flower-edged lane and suddenly, with little or no warning,
walk doubtfully beside a raging river? Will we walk fearfully
on the edge of a deep canyon one day, only to walk comfort-
ably through a green meadow the next? Will we travel dis-
couraged over rough terrain or journey hopefully over smooth
highways? Perhaps on any given day we will require both a
canoe to meander peacefully through gentle streams and a
lifejacket to tread anxiously in deep waters. Our journeys will
include most of these experiences, some uplifting, some chal-
lenging, and many mundane.

We will have days when we are lost on our paths or uncer-
tain at crossroads. We can solicit the help of our Guide, and
in his timing he will point his compass to proper paths, lead
through disappointments, and help us circumvent challenges.
We must believe in his ability to direct at forks, divert at
roadblocks, and smooth over pitfalls. We must trust him to
strengthen us to tread confidently into new areas. When we
journey through perilous places we must rely on his judg-
ment to guide us to safety. We must seek his encouragement
to help us overcome our doubts and fears. We must remain
close and listen to him with patient care. God our Guide,
who is wise beyond our comprehension, will orchestrate our

travels to exceed our expectations. We must trust our destiny to God and learn to follow him with the faith and courage of a butterfly.

Butterfly Courage

A simple unattractive caterpillar
Evolves into a beautiful butterfly in stages.
Moving bravely from lowly to lovely,
Transformed by the Creator over the ages.
Flying confidently with joy,
Flitting freely in God's guiding light,
Fluttering from flower to flower,
The butterfly flies without fright.
Our growing faith lifts the burden of fear
And inspires our trust in God's open door.
Living bravely with butterfly courage
Transforms us to fly freely and soar!

"I command you—be strong and courageous! Do not be afraid or discouraged. For the Lord your God is with you wherever you go"
(Joshua 1:9).

Sometimes we will struggle with the urge to turn away from God's path when we believe we know a better way. We will be tempted to follow a different guide who entices us to an alluring path that appears to be better. When this occurs we must remember our previous encounters with this guide have led us astray. We must trust in God's will for our lives and his faithfulness as we recall how much he cares for us, how much he longs to bless us, and how much he has already done for us. We can invite his wise counsel for our tough decisions and seek his clarity for our confusion. We must lay down our personal well-worn roadmap and trust God's divine map of enduring love to direct and light our path to contentment. We must trust in his wisdom to teach us his way and lead us on his straight and narrow path.

His Way

God's path is narrow while others are wide,

And though not the easiest, he'll wisely guide.

He'll light our paths; he'll lead to his star

And offer reassurance as he guides from afar.

He'll lead down the path he desires we take

And support each breath we anxiously make.

He'll guide our paths to peace-filled places,

Straight, narrow paths to brightly lit spaces.

We can walk all alone down life's challenging roads,

Stumbling wearily from our heavy loads,

Or trust in his wisdom, as humbly we pray,

Following his power, believing in his way.

"My child, listen to me and do as I say, and you will have a long, good life. I will teach you wisdom's ways and lead you in straight paths" (*Proverbs* 4:10–11).

We yearn for a serenity that is hard to define. We want to believe God will spread joy into our souls, even as we hurt. We look for the level of contentment that will enable us to walk with hope on troubled paths. We feel inspired to make the choice to follow God faithfully down the many roads awaiting us. We trust he will calm our anxious souls and still our pounding hearts with a peace that surpasses comprehension. We can invite him to carry our burdens and inspire a new tune with his love.

A New Tune

Reflecting fondly on flower-ridden pathways,
Finished with yesterday's weed-riddled roads,
Grateful for God's promise to carry my burden,
I ponder the bliss of a lighter load.
Smiling joyfully at the miraculous sun,
Singing inwardly by the light of the moon,
And peacefully dancing underneath the stars,
I seek divine intervention for a new tune.
Observing in awe God's wondrous beauty,
Gazing from afar into the valley below,
Resting my soul in the pinnacle of peace,
I'm amazed by his love I've come to know.

"I am leaving you with a gift—peace of mind and heart. And the peace I give isn't like the peace the world gives. So don't be troubled or afraid"
(John 14:27).

Can we believe he is a Captain who will guide to perfect peace that surpasses understanding and to jubilant joy that defies description? Can we believe he will inspire major hope in our difficult days, as well as our ordinary or triumphant ones? Can we believe the Lord will remove heavy burdens, reveal glorious times, and endow incredible memories? Can we trust him to sustain us through miserable trials, deep disappointments, and overwhelming sorrow? Can we have faith he will comfort us during the pain of illness or loss? Can we believe he will encourage us through the very worst of times? God who loves us and is faithful and kind will guide us with wisdom and grace.

Benevolent Grace

Our Lord's benevolent grace, sweeter than honey,

Bestows kindness, forever fervent and fair.

His tender mercies permeate our souls with peace

Like a pleasing fragrance filling the air.

God's joy floods into the tributaries of our hearts

Like water overflowing a river's defined space.

He recharges us with the courage to walk extra miles,

As he pumps our souls with his goodness and grace!

"I long to obey your commandments! Renew my life
with your goodness" (Psalm 119:40).

Yes, we can choose to follow our Captain as he reveals his bountiful blessings. We can believe that following God will exceed our expectations. We can appreciate the glorious splendor of his beautiful surroundings. We can revel in the joy of our inspiring circumstances. We can choose to rely on him while he moves with us through perilous places that require great endurance. We can choose to follow him on the ordinary roadways and remain hopeful the extraordinary will lie around the bend. We can believe that with each new experience hope will come for tomorrow's itinerary to be a route to joy. We can follow our Guide and trust that his path is the ultimate passage to peace. God, our extraordinary Guide, will bring us safely home.

His Divine Essence

We can focus on our Creator as we enter the darkened night
And sense his powerful presence dwelling in dawn's low light.
We can focus on God's grace to smooth our turbulent air
And feel his engaging love stirring us to grow aware.
We can let go of confusion and doubt as we draw near
And ask for faith to thaw our blocks of frozen fear.
His merciful reassurance will mend our splintered minds
And the love in his joy and peace will be the tie that binds.
Trusting in his sovereign power and forgiving face
Invites him to extend hope with mercy, love, and grace.
He'll repair our broken hearts with his healing balm
And subside our waves of anxiety with his power to calm.
We can focus on the goodness of God's loving presence
And trust our hearts to the cradle of his divine essence.
He'll inspire obedience and help our faith increase.
His mercy, grace, and love will beget joy, hope, and peace!

"'I am the Alpha and the Omega—the beginning and the end,' says the Lord God. 'I am the one who is, who always was, and who is still to come, the Almighty One'" (Revelation 1:8).

A meaningful relationship with God provides us with hope for contentment on earth and life everlasting. It isn't a matter of trying to find God, for he resides within our hearts. He awaits our understanding and belief that he is always available. We can choose to begin a personal relationship with him. The very essence of God can be seen, felt, heard, touched, and tasted in the world he created and in you and me. He is waiting for us to awaken to his presence, feel his presence, and invite his presence. As we draw close to God, he will draw close to us.

Remaining Faithful to God's Presence

Whether we journey over rough terrain or glide through life, contentment will be ours when we choose to remain in the presence of the Lord and trust in his promises for eternal life with him. We will receive God's life-sustaining hope, whether life takes us to pinnacles or pits, as we remain in his presence. He will lead us safely through life's landmines to absorb his ocean views in peace. He will return us to unexplainable joy, even during our trials. God will guide us to contentment regardless of how mundane life becomes when we focus on his presence. We can derive happiness on some level without a spiritual connection to God, but living outside his presence will not lead to the level of fulfillment that steadily sustains us day in and day out.

Awakening to God's powerful presence and inviting his friendship is the key to discovering contentment. Nurturing a personal relationship with God as we study his Word, communicate with him in focused prayer, and practice being in his presence every day is the key to growing in contentment.

Offering him our love with grateful praise and worship as we rely on him to guide us every day is the key to retaining contentment. The key lies within our hearts, where we can feel God's powerful light of unending love that will endure beyond time on earth.

Beyond Time on Earth

God will guide us to contentment,

Offering his wisdom and truths to assure.

His powerful light will never grow dim,

And the joy in knowing his love will help us endure.

God's indomitable, indwelling love,

His enduring compassion of infinite worth,

Unlocks the key to contentment each day

And remains with us beyond time on earth.

> *"And I am convinced that nothing can ever separate us from his love. Death can't, and life can't. The angels can't, and the demons can't. Our fears for today, our worries about tomorrow, and even the powers of hell can't keep God's love away. Whether we are high above the sky or in the deepest ocean, nothing in all creation will ever be able to separate us from the love of God that is revealed in Christ Jesus our Lord"* (Romans 8:38–39).

It isn't easy to remain faithful to God with life's endless distractions. It is difficult to focus when we are confused or anxious. We are distracted by sorrow and disappointment. We often experience doubt and fear during hardships. It is easy to ignore our devotion to our faith during boring or ordinary days. We grow lazy. We grow ungrateful. We grow complacent. So, how do we focus faithfully on a personal relationship with God? What is the key to being consistently faithful beyond the mountaintop moments? How do we remember to focus on God during ordinary days as well as in times of trouble or periods of success? How can we learn to focus on God consistently? What is the secret to putting God first in our everyday lives?

We grow in our faithfulness to the Lord as we develop a prayer life and study the words of the Bible. We mature in our faith as we praise and worship him. We learn how to be faithful to our Guide by studying the faithfulness of others. We can look at the life of Apostle Paul who was dedicated to spreading the Good News about God with unswerving faith, complete trust, and faithful obedience. We can reflect on Mother Teresa with her compassionate, kind, and exemplary life of service. And we can ponder the faithfulness exemplified by Brother Lawrence, a pilgrim who dedicated his life to being in the presence of God.

According to Brother Lawrence, who was born Nicholas Herman in France in 1611, the greatest secret of living in God's Kingdom on earth is in the art of "practicing the presence of God in one single act that does not end." He often stated,

God alone is capable of making himself known as he really is; we search in reasoning and in the sciences, as in a poor copy, for what we neglect to see in an excellent original. God himself paints himself in the depths of our souls. We must enliven our faith and elevate ourselves by means of that faith, above all our feelings, to adore God the Father and Jesus Christ in all their divine perfections. This way of faith is the mind of the church, and it suffices to arrive at high perfection. [2]

Brother Lawrence was raised with a strong faith and a great love of God. As a young soldier he was taken prisoner and was later wounded. He encountered many hardships but persevered in his faith. During this time Brother Lawrence had a specific experience of unusual clarity that placed him on a deeper spiritual quest. One winter, during a period of personal poverty, he gazed silently and patiently at a tree, barren of leaves or fruit, and grasped the extravagance of God's grace and unfailing sovereignty in giving life. Feeling lifeless like the tree, he realized God would renew his life as he does the tree each spring. The tree spoke to him of God's divine providence over creation. He became aware of the changing seasons as they represent God's faithfulness and unending love. Brother Lawrence began a life of expressing gratitude for the gift of hope and for his own rebirth by "practicing the presence of God in one single act that does not end." He spent the remainder of his life expressing his love to God by living with gratitude and joy in his ordinary world.

It was when Brother Lawrence became a helper in the kitchen of the Carmelite Order of Paris in 1649 that he became known for his simple, practical faith. He held high thoughts of God and meditated unceasingly. He believed it is the dedication to seeing God in every area of our lives that draws us close to him. Brother Lawrence felt communion with God in our busy times, as well as our quiet times, is what nurtures our relationship with him. He felt we must open up to God whether our experiences are ordinary, unusual, or miraculous. We must reflect on him even as we perform menial tasks. He suggested we invite God's presence when we wash dishes, make beds, or sweep floors. He teaches us from the example of his life that as Christians we have the ability to participate in an ongoing fellowship with our Creator. We must merely open our hearts to receive God and his loving presence. Brother Lawrence discovered that such devotion to God yields great joy. A joyful heart helps us remain faithful to God through life's ups and downs. Brother Lawrence believed we could draw close to God every day and experience him in all things.

Experiencing God

We don't have to visit the rain forest,
Frolic delightedly on a sunbathed seashore,
Or reach the pinnacle of a mountain
To have God's level of hope in our core.
We don't have to stroll in a rose garden,
Witness the glory of a breathtaking sunrise,
Or discover an inspirational rainbow
To experience the grace he never denies.
We don't have to ride ocean waves,
Stroll peacefully in a gentle spring rain,
Or hear the joy in a bird singing at dawn
To hold dear the love that lessens our pain.
We don't have to be wise beyond our years,
As righteous as an innocent newborn,
Or suffer from a broken heart
To receive the mercy God will gladly adorn.
Burrowed invisibly within our souls,
Resting within the recesses of our hearts,
And closer than the land is to the sea
Is God waiting with friendship to impart.

"Look! Here I stand at the door and knock. If you hear me calling and open the door, I will come in, and we will share a meal as friends"
(Revelation 3:20).

———————————————

Through the divinely guided experiences of Brother

Lawrence we discover that we will grow in our faith as we develop the habit of seeking God's presence every day. Our relationship with God will flourish, and our faith will ripen as we consistently praise and worship him. We draw closer to God through familiarity, honesty, and authenticity. Drawing into God's presence helps us recognize our heavenly Father's compassion when we hurt and find joy in him when we are discouraged. We can receive peace during confusion and hope during discouragement as we draw near to him. These revelations increase our faith. We grow spiritually when we give God our treasured time, our personal truths, and our authentic hearts.

God desires that we choose to follow him all the days of our lives. Our faith journey is a process of lessons that offer us the possibility to learn and grow. God created us with a great capacity to love and an innate longing to know him. He waits patiently for us to awaken enough to feel his powerful presence and hunger for his love. As we answer his call he begins a gradual inner transformation to help us become more Christ like. He urges us to listen and learn his truths that we might grow spiritually.

Our focus on our Guide suffers from life's distractions. Some days we are unable to feel his presence at all. We lose our way. We make wrong choices. We stumble and fall. We grow discouraged or disappointed. We suffer from grief and despair. God waits patiently for us to return to him. When we turn our eyes once again to the Lord he will guide us through our disappointment and comfort us in our sorrow. He will love us through despair. God whispers hope and inspires joy as we refocus on him. He settles an unexpected peace on us that is difficult to explain or comprehend. He instills trust and obedience as he leads us to his purpose for our lives. Whether we are in the valley, on the mountaintop, or at points in between, we are surrounded by God's circle of love.

Circle of Love

God encircles us with a fortifying love,
Surrounding us from dawn's first light.
He comforts with outstretched arms,
Protecting into the darkness of night.
The same healing love when we're broken
Is the grace in forgiveness when we err.
His sustaining circle of love abides,
Throughout the day, merciful and fair.
God, who created you and created me,
Loving each of us before birth,
Anoints our hearts with his encircling love,
Nurturing us for heaven beyond earth!

"For the mountains may depart and the hills disappear, but even then I will remain loyal to you. My covenant of blessing will never be broken,' says the Lord, who has mercy on you" (Isaiah 54:10).

Acquiring insight into God and his direction for our lives isn't always easy, but we do not have to memorize the Bible, attend a secluded mountaintop retreat, or wear ministerial cloth in order to grow with the Lord. As we experience God through praise and worship we grow in our understanding of who God is and how he works in our lives. We learn about God's character through prayer and the study of his Word. We acquire great insight into God's power, beauty, and compassion through nature, people, and our circumstances.

God urges us to goodness with lingering convictions. He nudges us to kindness with repeated inspirations. Sometimes he moves us to acts of righteousness through recurring thoughts, images, or feelings. Sometimes his messages come to us in our dreams. He whispers inspirations as we awaken in the night. He offers reassurance toward dawn. He instills hope at the start of a new day. He encourages us during busy or slow times. He enters our thoughts when we take a shower, walk the dog, or drive a car. He surprises us with inspiration when we gaze upon an exquisite orchid, a bubbling brook, or a towering pine. He moves us to ponder his supremacy as we look into a baby's smiling face, a teenager's tear-stained face, or a grandmother's lonely face. We sense his presence as we perform mundane tasks or important jobs. When we "practice the presence of God," eagerly attuned to his Spirit, we learn how to recognize the whispers of his will.

We can invite the promptings of the Holy Spirit anytime, anywhere, for God is, indeed, everywhere. Our quiet, focused moments of meditation are likely to be the most conducive to communicating with God, especially as we approach him with an open heart, receptive mind, and absorbent soul. When we draw close to God, he will draw close to us. He will be our armor of defense against guilt, anxiety, and fear. He will help us retain our capacity for joy. The Lord will be our shield against confusion and doubt. He will guide us from the path of discouragement to the path of peace. He will respond with whispering hope and lead us from despair. We can seek God's love and solace in our silence and trust that he understands.

He Understands

God understands the grief we bear;
He knows the pain we feel.
He sees the challenges we face
And the tears we try to conceal.

He holds us close in his loving arms
And whispers what he's all about.
He carries us through our sorrows
And relieves our burdens of doubt.
He lessens the weight of anxiety and fear
And helps us deal with life's demands.
He removes our wrongs, guilt, or regrets,
And through it all he understands.

*"How precious are your thoughts about me, O God! They are innumer-
able! I can't even count them; they outnumber the grains of sand! And
when I wake up in the morning, you are still with me!"*
(Psalm 139:17–18).

———————————

We have a tendency to rejoice and glorify God on the moun-
taintop, but we usually allow the bubbles of joy to drift away
when we descend. Although we may give God credit for car-
rying us out of the valley of difficulty, we repeatedly grow
fickle as our memories dim. In our boring or ordinary days
we often grow complacent toward God. Developing the habit
of praising God consistently whether we are resting on the
mountaintop of exhilarating times, walking in the valley of
hard times, or following the path of ordinary times provides
the armor we need to walk serenely and safely each day.

Focus on Me, My Child

Invite me into your fear-filled solace, my child,
And focus on me when alone in a crowded room.
Reach for my hope when you're grateful

Or when dreaded doubt accompanies gloom.

Ponder my presence as you stroll in your garden,

Drive your car, or occupy a church pew.

Turn to my joy as sorrow stifles your song

Or when you're contented, with troubles few.

Invite me into your serene reflections, my child,

And allow me to comfort when you feel bad.

Reach for my arms in the dark throes of pain,

And call on me, your Comforter, when you feel glad.

Focus on me while you prepare a meal,

And take me to the mall or the golf course.

Know that my hope is wherever you are

And for redeeming peace, I'm your ultimate source.

Take time to reflect upon my wisdom and power,

As I move you through troubles or boredom.

I feel what you feel and I go where you go,

And I will wait for you to yearn for my Kingdom!

"Your heavenly Father already knows all your needs, and he will give you all you need from day to day if you live for him and make the Kingdom of God your primary concern" (Matthew 6:32–33).

Ultimately, God promises time with him will be unbounded and unlimited when we trust and follow him. We can seek God in our ordinary days to avoid complacency. We can rely on God to help us through life's tribulations that have the power to shake our faith. We can rejoice with him in our triumphant times, understanding they will not remain forever. We can love him every day with praise and thanksgiving.

Soul-freeing salvation comes to us from his infinite love. A journey with God includes his healing balm of love, soothing salve of mercy, and sweet bandages of grace. It is a pilgrimage that offers restorative powers through the most amazing lifesaving devices known to mankind. God's incredible gifts of hallowed hope, perfect peace, and jubilant joy restore us to wholeness when we are broken and refill us when we are empty. God's life-transforming gifts are available to us when we awaken to his powerful presence. As we do, we will be victorious in life.

Reflections on Walking in God's Powerful Presence

In retrospect, I realize how readily available God was to me all along, but for many years I had a tendency to keep him at arm's length or remain in partial slumber. I was blessed to feel God's love through my beloved family and dear friends. There were fleeting moments by day, near dawn, or in the middle of the night when God gently called me by name. He came to me in my dreams and caught me unaware as I awakened in the dark. He beckoned to my soul in the garden as I saw his generosity in the beauty of a flower. He visited me at the seashore as I sensed his mysterious power riding the ocean waves. He whispered to my heart in the mountains as I beheld his majestic beauty from a lofty mountain vista. He was there as I walked in a valley amidst streams and wildflowers. He was present in the glorious rainbow, visible in the beautiful snowflake, and available in the sunshine.

For several years I traveled on paths of boredom, frustration, and confusion. My journey was primarily void of peace. I got lost on challenging courses as I chose paths that led to fear, doubt, and anxiety. I trudged past the Lord's directions to peace, and instead I used my own roadmap in search of special signposts that might point the way to life's perfect inspiration peaks and incredible joy stops! I continued to long for hope, and the peace that follows, as I visited the difficult stops along the way. I ignored God's guideposts that ultimately lead to fulfillment. I participated in the loss of my hope, the disappearance of my peace, and the theft of my joy. What was I thinking? Perhaps I wasn't. It is difficult to think or grow aware when you are partially asleep or in a fog, but this much I now know.

This Much I Now Know

I've communed with the Lord at dawn,

I've communed with him at night,

I've met him at a crisis point,

And he has smiled to make it right.

I've ignored God in the shadows,

I've ignored him in the well-lit way,

And though I've turned my back,

He's remained close throughout my day.

I've drawn close and I've pulled away,

And this much I now know:

When I choose to focus on God's presence,

Sweet contentment begins to flow.

"So now we can rejoice in our wonderful new relationship with God—all because of what our Lord Jesus Christ has done for us in making us friends of God" (Romans 5:11).

Although I chose God as my guide, my journey has not bypassed difficulty, excluded sadness, or avoided reality. My journey consists of victories and trials, and it requires strength and courage to persevere. I have grown in my faith journey, but still, sometimes I ponder the potholes that jar my confidence or intimidate my hope. Without God's guiding love and anchoring strength I am vulnerable to the joy-robbers of guilt, anxiety, and fear. I am more likely to lose my way and forget that I am never alone when I shift my focus from God's faithful presence.

Regardless of my day, I often grow anxious when I fail to focus on communicating with my best friend. When I take life for granted and wander aimlessly, I lose my way. When I am unaware of God's presence, as though in a fog, my joy and peace are easily shrouded from me. When I focus entirely upon the face in the mirror, I overlook the essence of God that surrounds me.

Face in the Mirror

When my focus is on the face in the mirror,

I search willfully for self-satisfaction.

When I lose sight of God's presence,

I grow vulnerable to sin's distraction.

When I focus on trouble without gratitude,

I live without joy and his hope I fail to see.

When my focus is on the face in the mirror,

I lose sight of the One who set me free!

*"Commit everything you do to the Lord. Trust him,
and he will help you" (Psalm 37:5).*

When I attempt to walk alone, the path is more likely to grow rough or dim. My private path consists of wrong turns, wasteful backtracking, and difficult curves. Sometimes I stumble. Sometimes I fall. Poor choices, strong self-will, and regretful mistakes spread shadows across God's well-lit way. Doubt, fear, and distrust try to find a place in my journey. I have to guard against indifference and complacency. There are times when my soul feels barren and my growth slow or nonexistent, and there are days I am like an impenetrable rock.

An Impenetrable Rock

Some days, like an impenetrable rock,

My mind is firm, unable to receive.

With my soul dry and non-absorbent,

I'm challenged to trust or even believe.

Impervious to the joy in gratitude,

With a heart too closed to discern,

I withdraw, hopeless and discouraged,

And God's love and peace, I spurn.

"When I had lost all hope, I turned my thoughts once more to the Lord.
And my earnest prayer went out to you in your holy Temple"
(Jonah 2:7).

I have gradually learned from my experiences that I am growing even in my dry spells. When I am faithful to remain in God's presence, he remains loyal to me. When I am faithful to draw close to God, I absorb his living waters of love. Life invariably holds challenges, but for me it is a blessed way to walk through life. I find contentment in his presence.

Prayer is a vital component of my faith journey. The Lord's Prayer, as taught by Jesus Christ, Son of God our Father, is a very meaningful prayer that reminds me of God's sovereign power. Another important prayer to me is the Serenity Prayer, whose author is actually unknown, although credit often goes to Reinhold Niebuhr (1892–1971), a Protestant theologian who used the opening lines in an address he gave in 1934.

The Serenity Prayer

God, grant me the serenity

To accept the things I cannot change,

Courage to change the things I can,

And the wisdom to know the difference.

Living one day at a time,

Enjoying one moment at a time,

Accepting hardships as the pathway to peace,

Taking, as he did, this sinful world as it is,

Not as I would have it,

Trusting that he will make all things right

If I surrender to his will …

That I may be reasonably happy in this life

And supremely happy with him forever.

"Don't worry about anything; instead, pray about everything. Tell God what you need, and thank him for all he has done. If you do this, you will experience God's peace, which is far more wonderful than the human mind can understand. His peace will guard your hearts and minds as you live in Christ Jesus" (Philippians 4:6–7).

The Serenity Prayer is a vital instrument in my quest for peace. It is a channel through which I may receive God's help as I try to surrender to his will. It is not always easy to discern what I can change in my life and what I cannot. Many of my circumstances have taken a long time to reconcile with God's peace. When I am patient he helps me understand my limitations. He helps me accept my responsibilities. The key for me to receive peace through this prayer is to surrender control of my life to God. A popular remark among Christians is "let go and let God." It is a powerful remark and made more powerful when I am able to put it into action. When I can process through the emotional strain of "letting go and letting God," it eventually brings about a sweet and liberating peace that elicits gratitude and results in joy.

The Serenity Prayer does not lead to a trouble-free existence, but it helps me persevere. Even as I grow anxious in my trials, adhering to the Serenity Prayer helps me preserve the peace I find in God. Although it does not necessarily come instantly, when I focus on God's blessings and repeat the prayer periodically, it offers hope for attaining moments of his perfect peace. Ultimately, the Serenity Prayer is a vital vehicle that helps me maintain contentment through Christ.

When I neglect my prayer life, my vision of God is blurred. When I lose my way in a fog, his wonderful blessings feel forever lost to me. When this occurs I must seek his presence and remember to listen, as well as speak. I must recall that communication requires listening as well as speaking. I must honor God in silence with focused listening. I must listen quietly and patiently with my inner ear for his sweet, subtle whispers that reside deep within my heart.

It is not easy to follow God with unswerving faith when I allow my circumstances to make me anxious, worried, or impatient. During these times it requires extra patience and self-control to focus on God. Although I do not always feel God's presence, still I can ponder his amazing grace and mysterious power. It is when I sit in silence before him to offer my love that I am the most open to his peace and receptive to his joy. When I refocus on God's willingness to help me, it is comforting beyond my words. My commitment to journey with God far surpasses my self-guided journey. It is reassuring to remember that he is closer than my very breath.

Closer

Closer than the air I breathe or thoughts I conceive

Is God waiting for me to awaken and receive.

Closer than the rosebud to the stem or roots to the tree

Is God ready to pardon my heart to set me free.

Closer than the sky to the land or the sea to the shore

Is God guiding my soul forevermore.

"But whenever anyone turns to the Lord, then the veil is taken away. Now, the Lord is the Spirit, and wherever the Spirit of the Lord is, he gives freedom" (2 Corinthians 3:16–17).

Much time has passed since I made my decision to follow God. I prayed for the sunshine of his love to bring hope to my gray heart. I asked him to offer peace to my anxious mind, and I implored him to spread joy into my hungry soul. Gratefully I now recognize God's guiding light of hope when I am lost. I experience his unspeakable joy, sometimes when I least expect it. His love shrinks my disappointments, as nothing else can. The peace I feel in God's presence is not only resting in my mind, but it is burrowed into my heart and lying deep within my soul.

Although my spiritual journey is still underway, I can see more clearly how prudent I was to commit to a lifetime of following God. My journey is an ongoing process, as I endeavor to be faithful to him through the pits, peaks, or plains of my life with praise and thanksgiving. When I consistently enter his presence and remain receptive to his guidance, I thrive. When I do not, I thirst. God's love for me inspires my love for him, others, and myself. No path could compare with this profound journey I chose to make with him. God is an extraordinary Guide who excels in all ways, in all things, and at all times. I know that I still have much to learn.

"So I run straight to the goal with purpose in every step"
(1 Corinthians 9:26).

Alphabetical Index of Poems

Endnotes

1   Awakening to God's Presence through People
     Mother Teresa, *The Joy in Loving*, ed. Jaya Chaliha and Edward Le
     Joly (New York: Viking Penguin, a division of Penguin Books USA
     Inc., 1997), 13–34.

2   Remaining Faithful to God's Presence
     Brother Lawrence, The Practice of the Presence of God (USA:
     Whitaker House, 1982), 87.